# SUCCESS WITHOUT COLLEGE

Laurie Brown is currently an arts reporter for the CBC's "Prime Time News," and is heard on the weekly CBC radio program, "The Beat." Previously, she was co-host and associate producer of "The NewMusic," Citytv's internationally syndicated weekly show, and a VJ on MuchMusic. In 1993, she won the Canadian Conference on the Arts award for excellence in arts journalism.

laurie brown

# Success without College

## Days and Nights in Rock & Roll TV

Penguin Books

PENGUIN BOOKS
Published by the Penguin Group
Penguin Books Canada Ltd, 10 Alcorn Avenue, Toronto, Ontario, Canada M4V 3B2
Penguin Books Ltd, 27 Wrights Lane, London W8 5TZ, England
Penguin Books USA Inc., 375 Hudson Street, New York, New York 10014, U.S.A.
Penguin Books Australia Ltd, Ringwood, Victoria, Australia
Penguin Books (NZ) Ltd, 182-190 Wairau Road, Auckland 10, New Zealand

Penguin Books Ltd, Registered Offices: Harmondsworth, Middlesex, England

Published in Penguin Books, 1994

10 9 8 7 6 5 4 3 2 1



Manufactured in Canada

**Canadian Cataloguing in Publication Data**

Brown, Laurie, 1957-

Success without college

ISBN 0-14-016536-3

1. Rock music - History and criticism. 2. Popular culture. 3. Music and society. I. Title.

ML3534.B76 1994 306.4'84 C93-094958-7



The chapter entitled "Whispering Pines" was originally published as an article entitled "Songs from the Bush Garden" in *Cultural Studies* Vol. 5 No. 3, October 1991 published by ROUTLEDGE.

Permission to reprint lyrics of "Peace Sells...But Who's Buying" granted by Theory Music/Mustaine Music.

for Taylor
who wrote the book of love

and

David G. Wilkinson
who wrote the book of friendship

# acknowledgements

thanks to Iris Skeoch for convincing me I could write the book, Cynthia Good for asking me to write the book, and Meg Masters for making me write the book.

# Success without College

"If you're not watching TV,
you're on TV."

Hadley Taylor, age 2½

# introduction

**i**n which we find out why
this book costs what it does

**t**here is nothing in the whole world so powerful as the swell of a rock song as it builds towards a chorus. Or when you can feel the chords mounting slowly up some steel grid industrial stairway, and then in your imagination Jimmy Page fingers the volume control on the guitar and lets it go. Or when Aretha rides the chord changes and the backbeat and gives you an "Oooh yeah" dead at the centre of your solar plexus. Nothing in the world can compare to that because it is made up of all the other good things in the world; it's a cry of joy and pain that is completely true, sexual, caring, life-affirming and right. In all those ways, rock and roll should be women's work. The best of this music speaks to women as forcefully as it speaks to men.

This book offers something a bit different, a woman's view of rock and roll. The manner of this book is to make connections between things, and to me that's essentially a female way of looking at the world. Of course, men can look at things that way too—lots do, and more should—but it seems to me that it's fundamentally female to try to "make it all cohere," as Ezra Pound once put it in a not very good play he wrote while incarcerated in the St. Elizabeth mental hospital in Baltimore. Call it some kind of mother-earth, Gaia principle if you will.

It is no surprise to me that the predominant political thrust in this so-called post-feminist age is towards environmentalism, which is by nature a theory of the interrelatedness of things. This same motive informs a lot of criticism today. Works of art are increasingly seen as part of a flow and not as individual spasms of creativity that can be viewed in and of themselves, as individual, mountain-top-achieving milestones. Perhaps the person that explained that best was John Steinbeck, through his character Mrs. Joad (the mother of all mothers!) in *The Grapes of Wrath*. In an unforgettable scene, she explains to her son how men and women differ. She says men treat life like a series of mountains to be conquered—it's a sequence of small achievements, all uphill or downhill. But for women, life is like a river. It moves fast and slow, bends and curves, but it just keeps on flowing. It seems to me that attitude is also one which is very sustaining, especially in art. Only art that takes in the big picture, that places itself in a larger context will last, and will be understandable to anyone other than the artist. Nothing that I can see—not the books I read or the art I see in galleries—stands alone. It is all connected with predominant popular cultural themes, even if it exists only to violently reject them.

What are those essential connections? That for forty years rock and roll has been and remains at the centre of pop culture in the West and the East; that is has informed every influential medium for the last thirty years, and continues to do so; that fashion, film, art, advertising, theatre, dance, charity benefits, window dressing, foreign policy, food styling, toy manufacturing, politics, intoxicant marketing, car design and, most important, TV are directly and demonstrably in rock and roll's debt; that rock is such popular currency that it has become hard currency as well, and corporate interests have exploited it to within an inch of its life, posing a serious threat to its remaining of any genuine value; and that, these near-mortal wounds notwithstanding, rumours of its death are just that.

Rock and roll has influenced TV. But TV rules. Increasingly, TV is the medium and filter through which we experience our music, and, therefore, the way that TV has influenced, rejected and embraced rock and roll will, I hope, be an instructive parable for the ways in which it's influencing the rest of our lives. I think that rock and roll has genuine meaning, whereas TV is mainly hollow commercialism. But while TV has no heart, it is not beyond hope, for if we keep it in its place, with our fingers firmly poised on the channel changer, we can make it do our bidding. Maybe, one day, even TV will be able to truly rock and roll.

# strange days indeed

in which we hear a story about green rooms, groupies and ground cloves

For many years my career has been caught in that hard place, a place a bit dank, sweaty and infested, between the forces of rebellion (rock and roll) and the forces of capitalism (TV). Unique training to be a correspondent in the next big political skirmish, if you ask me. It is a kind of no-person's-land, a demilitarized zone where the ceasefire breaks on the hour and half-hour. The best way to survive it is to have a big, fat, jolly laugh at the whole thing. The few times I didn't were the same few times I was badly wounded, but since I'm here to tell you about it, you can surmise that most often I hooted. At the moment, I'm an arts correspondent for CBC's "Prime Time News," but from 1985 to 1990, I was a video jockey, or VJ, for MuchMusic, and host of "The NewMusic" on Citytv in Toronto.

It isn't the kind of job you get trained for in any school. (If there is a kind of journalism school that teaches taking your job very lightly, I'd like to know about it.) When I looked around for a role model, none could be found. In the states, MTV VJs were a rehearsed, stilted bunch who knew little about music and, in their little TV studios, were about as far away from the genuine under-the-rock scene as they could possibly get. In Canada, though the Much VJs were generally more knowledgeable about music, there was never enough said about it for my taste. My personal agenda was to try to infuse into my stories an attitude that was one part smirk, one part anger, one part humour and the rest pure passion—exactly my view of what rock and roll is all about. But how to make it all fit on that small blue screen in your living room? Well, most of the time it didn't. Rock and roll is much bigger than TV, and night after night I found myself more interested in what was happening off-camera than what finally went to air. So, for your pleasure or edification, here's the unadulterated truth.

## the shoot

Order a beer and look for your cameraman. There he is, having a heated argument with the band's soundman. Since the only way the band is going to make it on TV is if the soundman lets us have a feed from their sound-board to our camera, this is not a good sign. My job is to find the band's manager and have him tell the soundman "These TV guys are all right—let them plug in." But the manager, Claude, is a jerk. That's nothing new. I'm developing a theory about people who make a living off the talent of others. Agents, pimps, managers, lawyers, publicists, editors and journalists, too—when you boil it right down, it's a pretty mean way to make a buck.

This particular manager is giving me his best power-play line in the middle of the dance floor. After all the grief he's put up with tonight, he's finally found someone lower down on the totem pole to give trouble to—me. I let him rant for a few minutes, during which time he gets a little bit of low self-esteem out of his system and tells us to go ahead and plug in. (He also clues in to the fact that if his band doesn't get any press attention on this tour, there'll be no next tour. And no job for him.)

## manager

Right now, the manager has got to get out of this club. He's been trying to get to a drug store for the last eight hours. He ignored the toothache for two days, dulled it with bourbon for a day, but now he really needs a dentist. At 11:00 p.m. on a Friday night in Toronto, he'll have to settle for a fistful of 222s. Five agonizing hours on the band bus from Montreal to Toronto, checking his grumpy band in at the discount hotel, checking out the grimy club and watching the load-in, waking up the band and getting them to the restaurant, dealing with this TV crew he knew nothing about—only now can he head out and hope there's a drugstore close to the club.

It's damp out and he feels cold immediately. The

city looks completely shut down. If only he'd done this last night in Montreal where he knew something would be open. He only has forty minutes max. By that time the first set will be over and Brett, the increasingly unpleasant singer, will want to start abusing the soundman. He has to be there to referee. While Brett is probably too smart for the business, he swears the soundman just emerged from the primordial sludge. And he didn't make that conclusion on smell alone. Tony is their fourth sound-dog on this lousy tour, and although he is abysmal at his job, the manager doesn't have the stomach to find another one.

He heads for a neon strip mall with a donut shop, a 7-11 and what might be a drug store. Thinking about the last soundman makes his tooth hurt even more. He was fabulous—but a maniac. Night after night the club would be empty by last set—highly unusual considering that's when the alcohol level of the audience normally moves the club into overdrive. But for two weeks the audience stopped dancing halfway through the second set and were leaving before the band returned. It took the manager another week to figure out what was happening. The little sound-shit was playing games. It was those monster equalizers he insisted he bring along. Depending on his mood, he would aim the overpowering, shuddering, low end of the music mix to hit the audience in the lower, middle or upper body simply by changing the equalization. When he was in a good mood, he aimed the sound right at the crotch, inducing some pretty hot dance-floor romances. But when Brett gave him a rough time, he aimed for the stomach, making the audience actually feel sick. Either way, people were scrambling to get out of the club and into bed. The manager never told Brett—he would have murdered the kid. Instead, he just left a note under the door of the sound-dog's room at the hotel in Halifax, telling him his gear was in the luggage-check and to be out of the room by 12:00 and not to touch the mini-bar, if he wanted to live.

Shit, it isn't a drug store—it's Earlene's House of Beauty. All those bottles of shampoo and spray in the window tricked him. He can't walk any further, the 7-11 will have to do. He hates 7-11s. Going through the doors he always catches sight of the height markers on the side of the door. They make him feel like a criminal—and a really short one.

No 222s. Just aspirin. He has been chewing them for days. Feeling desperate, he looks the cleaning fluids over. Cloves! The voice of his mother seems to emanate from the Drano bottle. Yes, put cloves on your tooth. The spice section only has ground cloves. That doesn't seem right. But screw it, it's all they've got. He buys it, passes small through the door and hails a $2.50 cab ride back to the club.

## laurie

The cameraman is finally shooting and I'm wondering who to blame for the camera clearance screw-up. The record company, who may have forgotten to tell the manager that it had all been okayed; or me, who may have forgotten to confirm with the record company, or, most likely, the manager, who is determined not to let some record company rep tell him what's going on with his band.

The next hurdle, and the most terrifying one, is the stand-up. I look at you through the lens of the camera and tell you just what's happening and why this story is important. This takes a lot of guts—not because of what I have to say, but where I have to stand to say it. In the middle of the club. While the band is playing. As hundreds of slightly inebriated, ultra-cool, hennaed heads watch. The cameraman turns on a highly unflattering light of searchlight strength. I am prepared for it, I shut my eyes, but all the carefully cool Robert Smith look-alikes don't. They are now looking like blind Robert Smiths. They're mad, and I'm embarrassed. Someone throws an ice-cube at me (I really hate this part). It's this situation that has made me into "one-take Brown." Nothing makes the memory keener or makes you work faster than the knowledge that the next ice-cube may be a direct hit. Or if you give them enough time to work up what little courage they've got, one of many goofy drunks will leap into the frame, ruining your take by screaming "HI MOM!"

The stand-up is over; the light is off. It is now possible to fade anonymously into the grimy, cockroached woodwork to watch the band—and the audience.

The presence of a TV crew at a live venue can do funny things to the audience. Even though a club may be packed with hundreds of people, with music blaring, it is a very private spot. It's too loud for conversation, making a club one of the few places where you can be surrounded by people, even people you know very well, and not be expected to do any socializing. Seeing live music offers a rare opportunity for thinking—letting your thoughts move wherever you want and wherever the music suggests. The lights are low, few people know you, you can be someone other than yourself. You can dance if you want to, or you can leave it all far behind. There are no demands on the audience; it's the band that has something to prove, and prove it all night.

But the equipment, the lights and the activity of a TV crew change that. The audience, as one, realizes their social event is about to be judged by a whole different audience—the one at home. They will be put on camera, and their faces will be read for clues as to the worth of the band. Were they cool? Did they have a good time? Were they a critical, thinking audience—or inebriated jerks? The pressure is on.

## groupie

Susan is the first of her group to notice the cameraman. She watches him weave his way through the solid crowd to the sound desk. He and the soundman exchange nods while he sets down his camera, tripod and equipment bag. Susan watches him fish a pocket flashlight out of his pocket and hold it in his mouth, illuminating the contents of his heavy bag.

Finally getting her beer from the bar, she shuffles sideways through the crowded club back to her clot of nanny friends in the corner. They are impossible to miss. All Scottish or Irish, all freckled and fair, all under twenty-three—they pull a lot of attention. They come to this bar at least a couple of times a month. Well known by the bar staff, they are a frantic table, frequently hysterical, with at least one alcohol victim and one weeper per evening. Even so (or perhaps because of it), Susan knows her table is the best thing going in the bar, and she feels sure the cameraman will think so too.

"Look, look! MuchMusic is here!" A high, short scream and they are all on their feet, dangerously tipping their table of beer while masses of hair spin in all directions trying to find the guy with the camera. Susan proudly points him out. They settle back into their chairs, excited that their evening is about to really take off. They aren't just happy for themselves, they're happy for their favourite band. They've stuck to this band like toilet paper on a shoe. They are always the first ones on the dance floor, the loudest clappers, and they always want another encore.

From the beginning, it was impossible for the band not to notice them. At first the guys were genuinely taken aback; anyone that enthusiastic might be slagging or teasing. But bit by bit their egos got addicted to the adoring behaviour and they gave in to the girls, talking to them between sets, even giving Susan a broken cymbal at the end of a particularly hot show, which the band knew Susan had helped happen with some inspiring dancing.

The fact that Much is here means the girls are to be vindicated for all the time and attention they've paid to their favourite band. Their taste in music is about to be recognized, and they feel sure the reason the camera is here has to have something to do with them. They all remember watching TV in their rented rooms when they first came to Canada. Before they found each other and the nerve to head downtown to a strange city bar, they spent many lonely weekend nights watching local TV. It was a good way to figure out what Toronto was all about. But now, they are going to be on TV. Not only will it look like they fit in, they will be the "in" crowd. Feeling fearless, they order a round of Kahlua and ginger ales.

## cameraman

Gregg has been in this club at least a hundred and fifty times in the last three years on the job. Just like the bouncer or the bartender, he has cultivated a clinical approach to his job, and the people who party at this bar are simply put there to get in the way of his work. Like the moves repeated night after night on the dance floor, Gregg repeats the same set of actions every time he sets foot in the club. After a year of practice, he can now get the forty-pound camera, a thirty-pound tripod, a hockey bag full of lights, and a small bag of tapes, batteries, light gels and microphones into the club in one trip. Taking the most direct route to the sound-board, Gregg lays them down in the same order every time. First tripod, then camera, hockey bag, then tape bag. He is constantly aware of the condition of his back and shoulder, the two things that could end this job tomorrow if he isn't careful. Straightening up carefully, no damage done, he nods to the soundman. They've never met, but they both know a lot about each other. They both have the same famous club stories, the same unbelievable road anecdotes, and they live the same strange hours. Like an old couple, they are compatible to the point that silence between them is not threatening, it's a mark of professionalism.

They both watch Laurie and the manager do their little power dance on the empty dance floor not caring who wins. The soundman has no feelings either way about letting Gregg plug into his system, he just needs the manager's okay. It's all the same to Gregg whether they shoot this band or they eighty-six the shoot and he reloads the gear in his car. Only when it is obvious that he is indeed going to be able to shoot does he take off his jacket and stuff it under the sound-desk.

Gregg is as pleased as Laurie that the stand-up is over. Working hand-held and quickly, it was done in two takes, and no one caught his blind side with an ice-cube. Now he is on his own. Other than a list of the three songs he is to shoot, all the decisions are now his. He shoots what he wants to shoot, whether it is a close-up of the bare foot on the kick pedal, the table of drunken girls in the audience or the sweat rushing down the singer's face—for the only time that evening, he is in control. Crouching on stage, headphones on to monitor the sound, looking through a small black-and-white eyepiece is how Gregg sees rock and roll, and he loves it this way. He decides what the TV audience is going to see of this band—and he knows that with his camerawork, he can make a statement as strong as any talking head.

## laurie

I have found a fairly unobtrusive corner to watch the band from. Picking my location in the club is very important. Pick somewhere too conspicuous and people will think your ego has taken over, and that you're in it for the glory. What they don't realize is that standing out in the open, I'm a much too easy target for ice-cubes. Another option is to stand behind the sound-desk, where no one will bother you and people will think you're afraid to talk to them. My style is to sit at the end of the bar, out of the limelight, and slowly suck a beer out of the bottle. Not totally unapproachable, but slightly forbidding nonetheless. (Thinking about it now, I probably looked like one of those silent lunatics you see at bars, sitting by themselves, silently seething with rage. Oh well, it cut down the number of jerk encounters, and I didn't want to talk, I wanted to watch the band.)

A live performance says more about a band than a biography or liner notes ever will. How they dress, who they emulate, how long they've been doing this—it's all immediately apparent. The age and condition of their equipment tells you how successful they are—I've learned to spot rental equipment several miles away. And I also have a pretty good score when it comes to predicting how long it will be before they break up. There is nothing so noticeable as a drummer or a bass player who has fallen out of favour. The rest of the band performs a musical freeze-out on the luckless member. No wonder—it's a difficult thing to tell a guy he's no longer wanted when he's probably donated (close to gratis) a year or two of his time and talent (however limited) to the band. One particularly tactful band waited until their out-of-favour bass player was tuning up in the rehearsal room by himself, then opened the door and threw in a cardboard box that had "YOU'RE OUT OF THE BAND" written on it. Rock and roll isn't big on social skills.

Another good sign that the band is about to break up is when a fistfight breaks out on stage—among members of the band. During one memorable gig, the fight started on stage (between lead guitarist and rhythm guitarist), but when the drummer started screaming that they were wrecking his kit, it moved through the club and out onto the street, taking the audience with it. Somehow I doubt that the band got paid that night, or that they ever saw each other again. They should have, on both counts, because they'd given the best show that the bar had seen in a long time.

I have the utmost respect for any band that is able to get it together enough to get on stage. What has to be done to get to that point is an unbelievable amount of work, especially if you're not independently wealthy. You're dealing with four or five people with different kinds of day jobs. Actually, you're lucky if they have day jobs. Usually there's one waiter and a security guard, who both suffer the night shift. Even more difficult than scheduling three or four rehearsals a week is trying to find a space to do it in. My personal list includes: unheated garages in February, the basement of a bicycle shop (just move four hundred old bicycle frames and set up, no problem), the basement of a doctor's office, or, my favourite, a concrete storage unit in the bottom of the Royal Bank Plaza in Toronto. People think that musicians enjoy grunge, but, in fact, they're like pigs. They don't like muck, it's just that they're not offered anything else. So if you're lucky enough to find the time and the space—and four other people who are at least occasionally in tune with you musically and who you like as friends, or can stomach as acquaintances—you are almost off to the races. But, wait a minute—who'll do the scheduling? Who'll print the posters and staple them up around town? Who'll organize the taping session so you have a tape to give to club owners? And who'll do all the follow-up and gig-booking? And last but not least, who has a younger brother who has nothing better to do than sit at the door of the club and collect the door charge?

This is what rock and roll is really about. It's the hobby bands, house bands, "first" bands that are doing all the work to make rock and roll continue. And they do it for the love of it. It's certainly not for the money they are getting, because after you pay the sound guy, the rental company for all the extra sound technology you needed, and the beer bill at the end of the gig, a very lucky night might put twenty bucks in each member's pocket.

Playing is what it's all about. And for me, listening to the band play live is how I do most of my research for the interview that will happen between the second and third sets (just before midnight in Toronto, since bars close at 1:30 a.m.).

Lyrics offer up some questions for the band, but attitude, audience reaction and just where my own mind wanders as I listen are just as important. I have learned to trust these initial responses as the honest ones and follow them in the course of the interview. Sometimes I am embarrassingly off-track; other times I'm able to connect with the band so that, by the end, we all know we've had some kind of conversation and not just an obligatory interview.

The time between the end of the second set and the actual moment we're ready to start the interview is a difficult time. Where to do it? The club's sound system is still cranking out some pointless and usually mood-killing recorded music. It's everywhere, from the owner's office to the dressing room. Rock and roll clubs don't have a green room, so more often than not I head to the washrooms. Granted, the sound is a little boomy with all that porcelain around, but at the end of the night it's pretty quiet, and a lot cleaner than the dressing room. But this is not the end of the evening, and the washrooms are far too populated between sets, so we lug all the equipment up to the roof. Too bad if it's cold and damp, the skyline is terrific and we can't hear the music, even if we can feel it through the soles of our feet. The cameraman sets up while I find the manager.

## manager

Sitting at the bar with an outdated book of Yellow Pages, a cellular phone, a bourbon and a bowl of ground cloves, for the last forty minutes Claude has been left blissfully alone while he alternates between phone calls to emergency dental clinics and shots of bourbon. After every shot of bourbon he dumps a couple of tablespoons of ground cloves in his mouth, closes his eyes and rests his head on the bar. At least Brett isn't on his case. Plenty of fans in this hometown crowd want a word with Mr. Hair and Teeth, and the news of the TV crew has the band pumped so full of themselves that for this brief and shining moment they're happy. This is what the PR on a life in rock and roll said it was supposed to be like. For the band, the last two weeks of bad gigs, bad sound, bad hotels and bad tempers are now just a "Spinal Tap" memory. Maybe for the band, but not for Claude.

The cloves are beginning to eat away at the insides of his mouth. He swallows the whole gluey lot down with another shot of bourbon, fully understanding that the time for barfing all this back up is quickly approaching. He stands up. Gripping the bar for a second he steels himself to the task of ripping the band away from that gaggle of girls they so graciously allowed into the dressing room. They must be a British volleyball team or something. He wonders how many of them he'll have to turf out of the bus two hours from now.

## brett

While the rest of the band is always pleased to play Toronto, their home town, Brett develops a noticeable case of nerves about playing the place where they started. It's far easier to convince family and friends of the band's importance and fame when they're on the road. At home, they are given a chance to make up their minds for themselves, and not having control over that bothers Brett. But tonight is great. Big crowd, TV camera, an interview, and their favourite groupettes. It looks like success, and Brett, better than anyone, knows how to play his part.

Dropping into the only upholstered chair in the dressing room, he drapes his leg over the arm, cracks a beer and winks at the girls clustered in the other corner. He has worked up an honourable sweat, but he smells good—a mixture of a week's worth of expensive hair spray and the requisite bohemian patchouli oil. While the rest of the band leans on walls talking with friends, Brett addresses the room as a whole—his audience for the half-time show. Proving the rock and roll clichés don't stop with the music, Brett pouts and postures to the crowd's delight, and to convince himself, for another night, that he is what makes this band great. Sweat and swagger. He's what rock and roll is all about.

## laurie

approaching the dressing room, it looks to me like half the club is in there, including a Scottish girls' field hockey team. Why not? The band is supplying the beer. Obviously their rider calls for imported, since everyone has a full Kronenberg in hand. The icy tub in the corner is slowly leaking water over the carpet and people are squishing around the eight by fourteen room. It's loud, but Brett is the loudest. Hell, if he's going to give them free beer, they're going to have to listen and laugh with him.

It's obvious some of the people perched on the edge of the cast-off couch have never been in a band's dressing room before. They have this "I can't believe I'm sitting in the dressing room talking to Brett" look on their faces. Other first-timers are wondering, "Do I just go over and grab a beer? Do I have to say something to Brett first? Or do I wait until I'm offered one?" Then they see an old dressing-room schmooze pro walk in, take a beer and go back out to his friends at the bar. Case closed—just get a beer before they're all gone.

Watching this scene of greed and glory with me is the manager. He's softened up considerably since our unpleasant first meeting. I judge from his breath that bourbon might have something to do with it. But there's another smell I recognize that I can't quite place. Too strong to be cologne, but maybe Crabtree and Evelyn have put out something very strange. As he turns to tell me he'll get the band and where do I want them, I can't help staring at his mouth. His lips, gums, tongue and in between his teeth are dark brown. It looks like what I imagine scurvy to be. I can't begin to think what to say to him. He heads into the room of plenty.

He's breaking up the party, corralling his boys, who scream with laughter at the sight of his mouth. He's in no mood to explain, but that doesn't stop the band from coming up with some wide-ranging possibilities about what the manager has been doing. Fifteen minutes later we're climbing up the fire-escape stairs to the roof. The band thinks it's a cool location; the manager thinks we're out of our minds. He huddles despondently on an old roof-tarring tin near the neon edge of the building trying to rub his teeth clean on a drink napkin. He has graciously given me fifteen minutes to get this over with.

No problem. This band has nothing to say. Just

full of interview jive. Trying to recreate a kind of Beatles' "first press conference in America" high-jinks, they fall badly short of the mark. This act is better suited to some sort of "Family Feud for the Intellectually Challenged." In my mind, this TV piece has just dropped from eight minutes to three. No matter how good the music is, if the interview is lousy, the piece is lousy. While good music, interesting haircuts and good looks can hold an audience for three minutes, good TV really does require talking head sound bites. Somebody has to say something somewhere along the the line, if a story is to make it to air.

I hear a sigh of relief from the cameraman and the manager when I cut the interview mercifully short. The band is cold, but exuberant. Their microphones are unplugged, and although we're not done yet, they all immediately rush to the edge of the building to look down at the closed car wash below. The drummer suggests they should make a video from up here, like on the roof at Apple. Oh brother.

## groupie

Susan and her friends are still in the dressing room going through the band's personal things. They are disappointed to find tooth-brushes, deodorant and hair spray. The only items truly worth shrieking at are a Maybelline zit-cover stick and a pair of pantyhose, both in Brett's bag. Then Wendy hits the jackpot, a stashed bottle of bourbon. A plan quickly takes shape. The bourbon, now six shots short of full, is the perfect interview prop. They must take it up to the roof and then ask to sit and watch what's going on. Unfortunately, they have to leave Karen behind in the dressing-room bathroom, the first alcohol victim of the evening.

## laurie

While the band cavorts around the roof, the cameraman quickly repositions the camera. It's time for a little routine TV magic, making this one-camera shoot look like a more expensive two-camera shoot. The camera is now where the band was standing, directed at me. Now I need to remember each question I asked, in what tense I asked it, and then look in the direction of the person who answered it. Remembering the questions isn't that difficult; re-asking them in a convincing manner is. The band comes back and stands back in their places, to get an over-the-shoulder angle on me. They try their semi-professional best to keep quiet while I re-ask the questions.

Questions done, the band tries to make a break for it, but we're not done yet. We need reactions. You know what I'm talking about—you see the band gaily gabbing on TV about whatever and all of a sudden a shot of the interviewer is inserted for about a second, and then it switches back to the band. A reaction. Usually a highly inappropriate one at that. Well, they're not there because of any narcissism on the part of the interviewer. They are there because the editor needs something to cut away to so he can edit the band's answer. This is where an acting background can help out. I simply try to run the gamut of emotions on reactions. Intent, sceptical, bored, smiling (open and close-mouthed), laugh (guffaw and slight chuckle), sympathetic (for the record company rip-off story) and last, but certainly the most important, the "Who is this guy trying to kid?" reaction (most commonly inserted in snotty English band interviews). Since each band member gets the full repertoire, this takes a bit of time, and the editor also needs shifts of my eye-line from one band member to another, to cover a quick camera pan when the drummer interrupts the more articulate keyboard player.

Bands think this is hilarious. I think it is embarrassing, and their barely stifled giggling doesn't make my job any easier. I'm about halfway through my reactions when the cloves become too much and the manager throws up over the side of the building (a reaction I've contemplated many times). The band explodes into laughter. We take a vote to keep going and get the reactions over with. I will dub in other, less offensive sounds back in the editing suite.

We're finished. As I'm wrapping my microphone cord up, the roof door flings open and the girls appear. Like candy out of a box they spill out onto the roof. The cameraman's eyes meet mine. Thank God we're finished—they would have been impossible to handle had they shown up during the interview. They deliver the bottle of bourbon to the boys, who look incredulously at its diminished contents, then swarm me with questions of when this will be on TV.

We're ready to go home. Equipment by the roof door, we take a last look around. The manager spread-eagled on the roof, head over the edge; the boys in pantyhose and tight pants teetering dangerously close to sidewalk oblivion; the girls shrieking with approval and reprimanding them maternally at the same time. That is the picture I take home with me. Another evening of rock and roll *verité*. On our way out I tell the bar owner he's got some lunatics up on the roof who he may have trouble getting down for the third set.

# the thinkers

in which we see that good music can
come from the head down or the hips up

Generally, nerves haven't played a big part in my job. I guess that's fairly unusual, because while the idea of meeting and talking to Mick Jagger is great in theory, if it actually happened most people would probably throw up or suddenly be struck dumb. (Even when people run into me on the street, often they can only blurt out "I know you," or "PowerHour!" repeatedly, remembering me as the host of MuchMusic's heavy metal specialty show.) Of course, it is neither the person nor the talent that stupefies the fans but the fame the musician carries around with him.

Fame has become exceedingly attractive and increasingly important in the last several years. I think the rock and roll generation has a preoccupation with fame, one that people over fifty regard sceptically. As

Captain Hook put it in *Peter Pan,* fame is "a glittering bauble" that can dangerously sidetrack a kid from what's important in life. I remember my own mother being repulsed by my fascination with it, fearing that one of the many nights I spent freezing outside the stage door at Massey Hall in Toronto, I would be swallowed up by that world of fame, never to be seen again.

My adolescent attraction to famous people came from the realization that while the talent of my favourite stars could always be analysed and explained over and over again, no one could explain their fame. Fame is, and always will be, a great secret. Even when it gets to such perverse dimensions as the kind of fame Madonna or Michael Jackson live with, it remains a mystery: why them? One thing we know is that fame lights on those with a magical combination of the common and the truly unique. The Mick Jaggers and Kurt Cobains of the world all share to a great extent the common man's psyche, but they all have a slice of true originality in their make-up as well. It has more to do with human nature than the sound of the music or the cut of their pants. Somehow these performers are able to offer us a package that we find complete. While they give us a taste of the exotic, we can also understand them enough to identify strongly with their image.

Another truth we know about fame is that we all want it. Fame brings with it the suggestion of great personal freedom, of being your own person, of being above the law and of being admired for the life you've chosen for yourself. Unfortunately the reality of fame is usually another story. Most of the truly famous people are slaves to their fame and carry it around with them like the chains of Marley's ghost. Keith Richards says, "Image is 50 percent you and 50 percent this long shadow of stuff you've done before that you can never get rid of." Imagine being defined at age forty-nine by what you did back in your adolescence!

The fascination with fame is certainly not just a pastime of adolescents who don't have it; there are plenty of musicians out there who forensically study the fame they have acquired. At the world-wide press launch of the Eurythmics' *We Two Are One* album in Cannes, France, all the journalists quickly realized that we were under scrutiny just as much as Dave Stewart and Annie Lennox were. Dave was taking pictures of every press gathering that weekend. For every picture taken of him, there exists a picture of the photographer in the process of taking his picture. With Stewart, strange bird that he is, it could have been just a smart-alecky retaliation to the enforced public display he and Annie had to endure—a way to hold on to a little of his private self—but I had the sense he was doing more than simply turning the tables on the paparazzi. I had the feeling he would be studying those pictures later, looking for something, some clue to the fame puzzle.

In finding his own way to deal with fame, Dave Stewart has walked a mile in some other famous shoes. On one publicity tour he was playing John Lennon: white leather suit, 1970s style, long hair and granny glasses. I remember sitting in the back of a white stretch-limo with him thinking he had gone completely barmy. He took me and my cameraman back to his hotel room, where he had hastily assembled a recording studio, and while we were there he wrote a song with us, his wife Siobhan on the phone from L.A. and a studio technician. A kind of sappy love song, it had global implications that suggested world peace was right around the corner, if we wanted it. Pure John Lennon. We shot the event and he directed, insisting on including shots of me and the cameraman. The final shot had him escorting us to the lobby and filming the people in the elevator who had recognized him. That afternoon would have been a waste of tape with a musician nobody knew, but Dave Stewart's own fame gave it validity (in spite of the fact the song he wrote wasn't very good). It was a successful day for me because I came away with a product that would give my audience more than they expected, and it was successful for him, because he returned to his hotel room feeling like he had had some control over the frenzied fame that manipulated him daily. But the whole event was really orchestrated by Lennon, who knew how to put a backspin on fame.

Lennon was one of the first to truly recognize rock's power and potential. One of the first pop stars to know global fame, he handled it with great intelligence. By 1969, finished with the Beatles but still in the not-so-still eye of a relentless media storm that exploited his many weaknesses, Lennon saw that this perverse power, fame, could be marshalled to some greater good. And some personal good, because Lennon was then able to resurrect a personal life. Leaving the world of rock and roll to take care of his newborn son, Sean, was Lennon's best comment on fame. He realized that the "responsibility to the audience" pressure was essentially false, and the only responsibilities he really had were to Yoko and Sean. What his idea of the greater good was remained somewhat mysterious, but it had something to do with telling people in mass mailings of Christmas cards that "War Is Over If You Want It" and singing "Give Peace a Chance" from inside a bag at Varsity Stadium or from a suite in the Queen Elizabeth Hotel in Montreal. In retrospect, I often think how futile it was, but how well-intentioned and gutsy. It was above camp; it was parodic of the very fame it achieved; it exploited fame and media exploitation. (The sad irony may be that the workings of fame are so widely understood that even an addled, pathetic case like Lennon's assassin knew that killing the lead Beatle meant the global front pages, even after scoring an autograph at the Dakota's doors.)

U2's Bono is also fascinated by the fame his music has brought him. He likes to use the Lennon model as well, but he identifies more with Lennon's weaknesses in dealing with renown rather than his playful, optimistic side. (I think Bono's grand experiment with the greater good fame can offer blew up in his face at Live Aid. He jumped off the stage and picked an audience member to dance with. He thought by personalizing the event and embracing an audience member, he could have the world that was watching by satellite throw down its guns. He said at the time it was an experiment that didn't work. He had overestimated his own fame and he didn't think it looked believable.) In the early days of U2, he embraced the darker side of fame. He was intrigued by the fact that Lennon, in the most famous band of all time, could write a song like "Help," while the world thought that he had it all. In fact, Bono focused so much on the down side of fame that the band had the reputation during the mid to late 1980s as being a real bunch of po-faced egomaniacs.

Back for the ZooTV Tour in 1992, Bono seems to have changed his mind about fame again, although the appearance of Salman Rushdie on stage at one show tells me his fascination with fame's walking wounded has not ended. (Obviously, Rushdie shares the same fascination.) Gold lamé suits, larger-than-life projections of himself—he seems to be solving the personal/public problem and is getting a little bit of fun from his fame. While it's obvious that the band still takes music very seriously, they have stopped taking themselves very seriously. In fact, the whole ZooTV tour seemed intent on deconstructing the U2 myth.

While Bono struggles to hold on to his personal self, he knows there are plenty of victims of fame in his audience every show. These are the John Hinckleys and David Chapmans of the world, sad people of a psychological underclass who feel that stars like Bono are both responsible for and a barrier to making them whole again. Or, in a strange twist of the mind, they trade identities with the star, imagining that the person on stage is the one full of inadequacies and sickness, the one who must be stopped. While this kind of sick fan is a reality for every major band, somehow I think Bono feels he is more likely to be sacrificed than any other major figure on the road today. He might feel that way because of ego, because his personality tends to lurk on the dark side, or it might be his sense of some kind of fateful, Irish luck. Standing backstage at a U2 show in Leeds, England, in 1987, I watched their manager, Paul McGuinness, scour the first fifty rows of the audience through binoculars for the entire performance. He was expecting someone or something, and he looked like he knew exactly who he was looking for. Meanwhile, the band played on, with Bono teetering dangerously at the edge of the stage.

The next time I saw Dave Stewart he had somewhat abandoned the Lennon ideal of greater good through fame and was trying on success *à la* Elvis Presley. White sequined suits were the order of the day, with black pompadours and over-the-top guitar moves, executed without a moment of self-consciousness. He was experimenting with the limits of his fame. A risky business—if he had miscalculated, he would have been laughed off the stage. But he wasn't; fame carried him. And while I like to think he was laughing himself silly at his ridiculous antics, the audience took it all in without a cynical or critical thought. In their song "Angel," from *We Two Are One*, Annie sings "I believed in you, like Elvis Presley singing Live from Las Vegas." Dave was trying to find out if his fame would let him go that far and still be believable.

Today, looking at Elvis, *Live from Las Vegas*, it's hard to connect with anything in that performance but fame. Everything else, physically, mentally and musically, had crumbled away under the weight of his popularity. Stewart calls that concert "classic music history." He sees it as the moment that "the powers that be realized millions could be made off music." They had turned Elvis into a "merchandizer's dream—there was nothing left but marketing." While the dress-up factor in the Elvis parody must have been fun for Dave Stewart, the ultimate message may have been that his talent now has very little to do with who he is and why he is famous—a sobering thought that has sent more than a few musicians over the edge.

The desire for fame is something musicians have in common. Many don't want fame for the money or the glory it can bring—they want people, and lots of them, to hear their music. They have an irrepressible urge to communicate. They are not creating this music to satisfy themselves; they do it because they think they have something people need to hear.

There seem to be two styles of famous rockers. One type comes from inventing your turf and then sticking to it. The Rolling Stones are the prime example. No matter who they work with, how the music changes, what their lifestyles are, they will always be the bad boys of rock and roll. The other type of fame thrives on change: Bowie, Madonna, Michael Jackson and Prince fit this bill. Their fame has endured because of their ability to continually reinvent themselves. To keep one step ahead, to keep the image moving, Madonna is exposing her breasts to everyone in the world one moment and clutching a teddy bear the next, while Jackson has physically recreated himself so many times his face is in danger of falling off. Change is essential in order to maintain their fame. This fame is connected to our politics, our values and our way of life, and none of these things remain the same for long.

We need to see the changes we have absorbed in our everyday lives reflected in our modern-day heroes. Pop stars must keep up with the rest of society or be left behind. Hammer's fall from grace is a prime example. He was at the height of his career in 1991, but in 1992, a mere year later, the same moves and crass, fabulously expensive publicity stunts that had propelled him to the top were alienating him from his audience. He failed to keep step with recessionary times.

I think Madonna, for all her prize efforts at media manipulation, knows little more about fame than the rest of us. She simply knows how to sell herself (a commodity the rest of us seem to be addicted to), and she knows we covet her fame, so she flaunts it in our faces. She's become a code word for our age, a universally understood expression of the 1990s. She's a single representative of a boatload of our feelings, and the fact that perhaps 50 percent of us dislike Madonna intensely lets you know what we think of ourselves. The person we choose to bestow fame upon is always a reflection of ourselves. A star who evokes strong feelings of both love and hate is a truer reflection of the zeitgeist than one who lacks legions of rabid detractors.

If fame is one eternally intriguing topic for musicians and journalists alike, then the origins of talent is another. When interviewing the truly great performers and songwriters about their creative talent, I sometimes get the feeling that there is another presence in the room. When it comes to creativity or inspiration, many exceptional musicians will tell you that they don't own any, can't summon it up on command; they consider themselves a medium through which their muse operates. They speak of their talent as an on-again, off-again friend, a mysterious acquaintance that cannot be counted on. Van Morrison, John Hiatt and Joni Mitchell have all said as much. That's when they speak of it at all: the whole thing sounds so spacey that most musicians would rather skip the topic altogether. These are the non-thinkers, the organic musicians whose love of playing overrides everything else. They operate without much of a critical sense and are instinctual about everything. They'll play with anyone, anytime, and have a great time doing it. Eric Clapton, Mark Knopfler, Keith Richards come to mind. By playing constantly, the odds turn in their favour that they are going to hit on something great more often than the player who won't pick up his instrument until he knows what he wants to say.

But there is another school of musicians that could tell you just about everything about the way they make their music. These thinking musicians work from the head down and leave nothing to a temperamental muse. They will tell you a good song comes from plenty of hard work; it's craft, not good luck. Songwriters like Sting, Bryan Ferry, Pete Townshend work that way. Even so, these artists are just as reluctant to talk about the process. It's not the rock and roll thing to do. The public code of behaviour for rock and roll demands that these songwriters must not take themselves or their creativity too seriously. It's supposed to be a natural, knee-jerk kind of occupation, one essentially focused on adolescents, nothing to get all uptight about. Writing a great rock song demands as much talent as any other kind of art, but even the intelligent, thinking musician finds himself in a difficult position when pestered by interviewers like me to describe just how he does his work. While writing a great rock song demands great skill, the end product nevers flaunts the thought process that went into it. When it does, the results are truly terrible, in a delicious, "Spinal Tap" kind of way. The pompous symphonic contributions of Procol Harum, E.L.O. and Pink Floyd in the 1970s are wonderful examples. The bad baroque of rock and roll, their music suited the times, but thankfully it has mostly remained buried in that fuzzy-headed decade.

In the 1990s, the old laissez-faire attitude to pop writing seems to be changing. Maybe because rock and roll is old enough now to have its own classics, or maybe because the most talented of the bunch are now in their forties and fifties, rock is finally able to take its songwriters seriously. That Elvis Costello can release *The Juliet Letters* with the Brodsky Quartet in 1993 marks a new level of maturity for rock and roll. Sure, some say Costello was taking "time off" to do some "serious" music, but his response to that is that he's been serious about every piece of music he's written. The critically acclaimed work of David Sylvian (ex of Japan) and Robert Fripp (ex of King Crimson) also help chart a path of new credibility for rock and roll composers.

That the songwriting talents of Eric Clapton have suddenly been rediscovered and have propelled him into near sainthood also speaks to the maturity of rock as a musical form.

The barriers between so-called "serious" classical music and rock and roll are coming down. As the Nigel Kennedys of the world have demonstrated, classical music contains the same passion as rock and roll, and the truly gifted talents of the classical world live like true rock-and-rollers—for their music, and on the edge of society. While rock and roll can't yet boast the staying power of the classical repetoire, it has outlasted any other form of popular music in this century.

While younger musicians, in what seems to be a mad rush to break down the strict boundaries between musical styles that the industry created for itself in the 1970s and 1980s, are pillaging their parents' record collections to find material for their first jazz record, others are creating new music to reflect this newfound maturity in the rock world. While it's great to hear Sinead O'Connor sing "Bewitched, Bothered and Bewildered" (a truly fitting choice), it will be far more interesting to see what she creates on her own outside of the rock world. It's the new music created by artists like John Cale (ex of Velvet Underground), Kate Bush and k.d. lang that truly intrigues me. Raised in the pop world, these artists have pushed the envelope and given rock more air space, and these are the people to talk to. Cale takes the best of new music to mix with his rock sensibility, Velvet Underground *à la* Philip Glass. Kate Bush, a technological wizard, miraculously mixes the organic (voice and Celtic tradition) with the manufactured. And k.d. is breaking new ground in what was taken for dead, middle-of-the-road mainstream music. She is reviving it nearly single-handedly.

The ability to get close to some of these people and to try to find out just how connected they are to their talent is the best and most difficult part of my job. These are the artists who make songwriting their lives' work. It's not recording, producing and touring that are keeping them in the music business, it's finding, and finding again, those precious moments of creative inspiration. Bryan Ferry grinds away at work daily, hoping that ten awful days of writing might inspire one great day. None of this school seems to wait around for inspiration to hit. They have to be in shape for songwriting and ready for the inspiration when and if it comes. That means having a place where day-to-day life does not intrude (either Mustique or the laundry room will do) and keeping their heads full of big thoughts and big feelings. They figure it's their job to experience everything they can to help fill the songwriting databank. That's why U2 went to Ethiopia to see starving children; that's why Joni Mitchell has done drugs; that's why Elvis Costello and Tom Petty go as far as admitting they purposely mess around with the lives of the people they love to keep their emotions rubbed raw. It's all to keep the creative coffers full.

Songwriting uses the in/out tray mentality—no input means no output. While you don't have to live the blues to be able to write a good song, the best artists feel the need to reach the limit at either end of the emotional spectrum. They're not afraid of sinking down in depression or experiencing the ultimate high. All seem consumed with a curiosity about how other people live. Their interest is directed not so much to the accountant in the suburbs but to those living on the edge, the great percentage of our society that, living outside the tiny bands of respectability, is judged "abnormal." From the fanatically religious to the desperately depraved to the politicians of the day, you will find musicians dabbling in the lives of many fringe-dwellers because they want to know what's possible, what's really happening. David Byrne and Eno recording people speaking in tongues, the Beatles jetting to India to sit at the feet of Maharishi Mahesh Yogi, Daniel Lanois immersing himself in the voodoo culture of New Orleans: these artists seem to be on a quest for the unusual. The truly great musicians have a curiosity that overrides their own morals and a willingness to be taken anywhere. These are the artists that bring us great, lasting songs. Songs that start in strange, far away places and end up being sung, by us, in our showers and our subways.

## david byrne

The two times I remember feeling real fear were when I met Bryan Ferry and when I met David Byrne—Ferry because he was my idol, and David Byrne because I was overwhelmed by his body of work. I researched for a week and still didn't feel like I had a grip.

I was to interview Byrne in Chicago at the release of his movie *True Stories*, his 1986 directorial debut. The interviews were stacked back to back—always a bad sign, meaning time restrictions and an exhausted interview subject. To a reporter from "The NewMusic," having to do an interview in a hotel room means failure. There is nothing interesting about looking at a lamp, a couch and a plant for twenty minutes, no matter who is on camera.

Chicago is one of the architectually most diverse cities in the United States, and I was determined not to let a backdrop like that escape. So I ran a reconnaissance mission through the Water Tower Place, where Byrne was staying. Since the interviews were twenty minutes each, with no time in between, Byrne would not be willing to go anywhere out of the hotel. But what about the roof? I had to get David to go up to the sixtieth floor, walk through the men's gym change room, walk around the pool and meet me on the roof. He did.

It was a very hot day and Byrne and I were wearing the same thing: white collarless shirt and navy-blue vest. Now this might have been disastrous. Some musicians would have run and changed immediately; the idea that the interviewer could have come up with the same fashion statement as the star doesn't do much for the old ego. While it made me slightly uncomfortable, he said nothing.

Byrne had created for himself the perfect antirock persona: the total nerd. Can't sing, can't dance, terrible hair. In the early days of the Talking Heads, the mid-1970s, his aim seemed to be to become the first invisible front man for a band. He hated all the gimmicks of rock and roll, the spotlights and smoke bombs. He said the Talking Heads didn't want to trick anyone, so he stripped away all the usual trappings. He refused stage lights and insisted instead on blazing white lights across the entire stage. He didn't want any action of his singled out; he didn't want to be seen as the star. He wanted people to notice that there was a band on stage. Yet for all his democratic gestures, Talking Heads was definitely a Byrne creation. So was his halting, self-conscious approach to singing. Singing into a tape-recorder over and over again, he would pick the most unnatural and interesting emphasis and phrasing for each line, and from the many takes he would construct a style.

The songs were always about ordinary things. He never wanted his lyrics to say too much, yet by concentrating on everyday objects and everyday tasks, he bestowed great importance on them. David Byrne gave us an alien view of American culture, seen as if for the first time, isolated and under a magnifying glass. His fascination with everyday life and the tools we use to live it showed up the silliness and narrow-mindedness of the world around us. You'll find the word "house" in more songs by Byrne than by any other artist. But while he understands the import of that word in American culture, the psychological meanings, the American preoccupation with property and the fact that "house" is where the heart is, Byrne tells me he likes the word because it sounds so funny when you sing it. There's that old rock and roll attitude of shrugging off the upfront thought that went into the music. In actual fact, his writing style usually starts from a state of order; then he shuffles the deck, creating the disorder needed for rock and roll.

For all his simple answers and protestations, David Byrne is known as rock's thinker. That his area of specialty happens to be an anti-intellectual middle American culture, where he feels the real creative force of the country comes from, can't disguise the fact that Byrne's music with the Talking Heads happened from the head down. His minimalist use of language, reducing every word to its most simple and literal meaning, also made up a great part of the character he created for himself. That makes interviewing Byrne very difficult. Irony, humour and sarcasm don't compute with Byrne. I would ask a question, and it was as if he visualized what my question would look like written down before he proceeded to answer in his very literal way.

Byrne is one of the only writers in rock today who does not write from personal experience. One always assumes the artist is creating from within, but Byrne proves you don't have to get personal in a song; instead he writes about everybody. He thinks of his music as a kind of Marxist commodity, art for the masses, rock for the people. It amuses me no end to find out that in 1974, while at the Rhode Island School of Design, Byrne was trying to work out a "Nielsen Rating System for the Arts." Through computer terminals, multiple choice and yes/no questions, he wanted to develop a system that would connect visual artists to the people who were moved by their work. This would be a system everyone had access to, and by answering questions like "Do you like straight lines better than squiggly lines?" and "Would you just as soon watch stuff on TV?" the computer would put consumers in touch with the visual art style they would most likely enjoy. Byrne has always believed that music and art have a real and practical value to people's lives, and that once we acknowledge that fact, they will be consumed more like a product you would pick up in a grocery store than one behind a glass wall at a museum. True U.S.-style consumerism.

I was most interested to find out what lurked behind his fascination with the tabloid mentality of middle America. Was he laughing at the people he was writing about? Was *True Stories* simply a cruel joke about a segment of weirdo population that didn't know he was laughing at them, or was there something else behind it?

He said it wasn't a cruel joke. While the wacky tabloid stories about women giving birth to green peppers did make him chuckle, it was the sense of conviction and belief of the readers in these magazines and the inner strength they got from their faith in these stories that Byrne found admirable. Some may call it blind faith, but it was his interest in that kind of total conviction that I think lead him to Brazil to make his documentary, *The House of Life,* about the Candomblé religion. The film is filled with people in trances, and their spastic dances are very similar to Byrne's own odd stage movements, although Byrne says his "dance" comes from religious "fits" much closer to home—the U.S. Bible belt.

After the interview, we ended up in his suite, where I was to interview Pop Staples (who was also in *True Stories*). While I was there I noticed a stack of *Time* magazines with Byrne's picture on the cover. They had hit the streets while we were talking on the roof. The idea that had been running around my head during the interview suddenly made more sense: David Byrne as a kind of Norman Rockwell for the end of the millenium.

The next time I met him, in 1989, David Byrne was a very different person. He had just released his solo album, *Rei Momo*, and he was on tour with a Brazilian band that had both him and the audience sambaing in the aisles. The absolute pleasure he was experiencing on this tour was something I had never seen on a Talking Heads tour. I asked him if he was working from the hips up instead of the head down, and he agreed. Rather than do all his thinking up front, and then try to find the pleasure and the passion for the music later, he had reversed his priorities. Confident that he could make it gel and eventually mean something in the final mix, he was letting himself (and his audience) have a little fun.

His halting, self-conscious manner was mostly gone, and even the lyrics for the new album didn't sound like Byrne. The first line on the record was "Sometimes I get horny"—slightly out of character for him. He just smiled and said, "I guess I can't go on playing the same character my whole life."

I see that change in Byrne as a survival tactic. There has to be a balance between work and pleasure in making music, and at times, while the music was always interesting, I got the sense that the Talking Heads were not getting a lot of pleasure out of it. Now that Byrne has unburdened himself of the band, the prospects for seeing and hearing more of his work in dance theatres, films and concerts are even better.

## kate bush

the only time I have ever had to submit my questions prior to my interview was for Kate Bush in 1987. Her record company would fly me to London to interview her at her brother's house, but only if my questions were submitted and approved (presumably by her) beforehand. I knew she didn't like interviews but I wasn't sure why. Perhaps it was nerves, the invasion of her privacy, an inability either to talk about her music, or suffer fools. Anyway, my questions were approved and I flew to London.

Her brother's house was about an hour outside of London—a huge old estate he was desperately trying to stop from crumbling into the ground. Kate appeared, coolly but politely warning me that the twenty minutes I had flown across the ocean for would never amount to anything more than twenty minutes.

My admiration for Kate Bush is immense. First, she is a singer with a four-octave range who found a way to use it in rock music. Second, she's a kind of hippie Celtic witch; she has brought all her ancestors' history, literature and music with her on her pop musical trip. Third, in spite of the ancient history in her music, she was a product of the latest in sophisticated sampling technology, one of the first artists to truly tame the Fairlight synthesizer and make it fit her requirements, rather than build ideas around the machine. Fourth, I'm amazed by her ability to integrate modern dance into rock. I don't think her dance for the video "Running Up That Hill" has been equalled by anyone yet.

Even though she had seventeen hit singles between the ages of seventeen and twenty-seven, her connection with the rock and roll world has always been tenuous. She has never played live in North America, and at home, very rarely. She is considered somewhat of a hermit, a bit of a mystic working away in her own studio and keeping the outside world as far away as possible. Part of a very close-knit family that both manages her and plays on her records, she is rarely seen in public. She knows she doesn't really fit the rock world that nonetheless has embraced her music, and I get the sense that she is not confident in her role as "outsider." The video she and Peter Gabriel did together sums up the position they both hold in the rock world, I think. For the entire song, they are holding on to each other for dear life while encouraging each other, "Don't give up—you're not the only one."

My big surprise in the interview was how many times she brought up the subject of money. The cost of recording, the cost of making a video—she made me think her musical product was solely the result of how much money she spent on it. She also repeatedly lamented how little time she had to work on the music and videos. Time and money were her principal concerns—hardly the free spirit I had learned to love from her music. Yet here was an artist who never had to tour, never succumbed to the promotional blitz that most musicians are forced to go through on the release of their albums, and never showed up for photo opportunities. If there is any artist who should have plenty of time it's Kate Bush. Owning her own studio should take away any kind of pressure she would feel in the studio because of cost—no need to punch a time-clock. How could an artist of her stature be so worried about how much money her record cost?

Her concerns seem trivial when put up against the kind of topics that she writes about. In her songwriting Kate Bush is definitely an uneasy person, whose constant questioning of who we are and why we are here makes for successful music. But in day-to-day life, she comes across as an overly sensitive, even obsessive person with a complaint about everything. She suggested to me that all artists are uneasy people, and I agree, but Kate Bush struck me as one of those artists who, rather than having trouble keeping in touch with her creative side, is troubled dealing with anything other than that.

The interview was shaky at first, but once I brought up the subject of the style of modern dance she has brought to her music she began to talk willingly for the first time. She thinks of music without dance as an unfinished product. Only when she can dance to her music does the creative circle complete itself. She's right: music is to dance as gas is to car engines—it makes things go. Both music and dance make designs in time. But putting modern dance on video is another story altogether.

There may be something inherently alienating about putting dance on TV. Some dance purists will tell you that the whole point is to be in the same room as the person sweating out their emotions, that two-dimensionalizing dance for the tube makes it flat and lessens its expressiveness. For Kate, dancing on video serves to help humanize the technology she uses, for dance is people, flesh and blood. It's not objectified, like music or painting, it's alive. The more technology Kate Bush uses, the more important the dance becomes to counterbalance its effects. The trick is to discover a way to shoot dance for the cathode-ray tube that doesn't rob it of its impact. I think she achieved that with "Running Up That Hill" (her biggest hit since "Wuthering Heights," the record company forced her to change the title from "Deal With God" to get airplay). While the dance in the rest of her videos consists mostly of exaggerated posing to the music ( a kind of wide-eyed, mimed version of the song), "Running Up That Hill" was "serious" modern dance. Choreographed by Michael Clarke, a Brit punk with ballet training and a sense for the absurd, the clip showed us that Kate can truly dance, and that dance on video can offer a much more accessible intrepretation of a song than the tired old literal versions we've been getting for ten years now. After all, rock music translates to the physical with no effort at all. Rather than have some TV commercial director decide what the song means and present me with that definitive version, a dance video means my own interpretation of the song remains intact, and I'm offered instead, through human movement, an abstract and complementary illustration.

Kate Bush is a disciple of the famed Scots choreographer Lindsay Kemp. (Her song "Moving," on *The Kick Inside* is about him.) He and Kate believe that dance is a more important form of expression than music, theatre or literature today. And they might be right. If you want to find art on the leading edge today, modern dance is the easiest place to find it. Yet it is considered a minor art—its intuitive value is high, but the financial reward and recognition in our society is very low. I saw Lindsay Kemp's tour of Canada in the 1970s. It featured his version of Jean Genet's "Flowers" and was a semi-mystical, almost psychedelic romp of white-faced and harlequined men rappelling around the stage. It felt more like the dangerous side of rock and roll than anything I had seen on the concert stage in quite some time.

Kate also gave her ultimate dance performance in "Running Up That Hill." While she did not say why, I suspect it would be her age. That she waited until 1986 to finally introduce her audience to her serious dance side is a great mistake. While she privately danced in her own studio for years, she waited until modern dance had more exposure before seriously attempting choreographed dance in a video. By then, at 26, she felt as a dancer she was past her prime. Surprising that the woman who expanded the boundaries of rock by light-years didn't feel she could bring modern dance into that arena at the same time.

Our twenty minutes was up, and after cajoling her into going outside to get a shot of us walking together in her brother's wild garden, we said goodbye. The week before I had interviewed guitarist Michael Hedges, and he had given me two of his CDs for me to give her—he was a huge fan. Surprisingly, she was overjoyed, although she hadn't heard of him. She said no one ever gives her music, and she doesn't get to hear much. She wanted to play them immediately. (I wonder if Kate Bush has ever been in a record store?)

She was gone, and we were packing up. Her brother, John Carder Bush, presented me with a book of photographs that he had taken of Kate when she was growing up. It seemed to me like a gesture of warmth that he knew his sister couldn't provide. He published this book in 1986, and the photographs do more to explain who Kate Bush is than any interview ever will. Even at eight years old, Kate Bush looked at the camera with the eyes of her Celtic ancients, a kind of pre-Raphaelite child who would always remain uneasy in this world.

## david bowie

I was in London to cover Island Records' twentieth anniversary when I got a phone call to go to Paris to interview Bowie the next day. I had never met him before, and had no research or preparation. At first I panicked. Bowie's work has sustained volumes and volumes of criticism and conjecture, and here I was having to wing an interview. But I have been a fan since *Hunky Dory* in 1972 and told myself I would just have to trust my instincts. There's a lot to talk about with Bowie, and it doesn't have to be music. His music is full of dance, his live shows are crammed with plenty of theatre; he paints and he acts. He understands media, and as I was about to find out, my presence was hardly required. He knew how to give good TV.

He was taking his Glass Spider Tour across Europe and had been getting creamed by the press. The

British press were tough, as usual, and he was having grave doubts about bringing this circus to North America. The incredible expense of this tour made it imperative that he fill stadiums, so in between shows in Paris, he was hyping the show to the North American press.

We travelled to a park on the outskirts of Paris to see the show. The crowds were unbelievable. The cameraman and I were positioned at the sound-desk, halfway back from where we were to shoot the first song and watch the show. By the time the show started, the scaffolding of the sound-desk was threatening to collapse from the crowd pressing around us, and the wooden plank floor was littered with passed-out fans who had been lifted up to us. There was no way to get them to first aid, and no way for us to get out. I had to make a decision: would I spend the show thinking about what kind of real danger I was in, or ignore it? A real no-brainer: ignore it.

There was so much to see, it truly was like a three-ring circus. Bowie is one performer who choreographs every single movement on stage, not so much to impress with dance steps, but for the video cameras that accompany every show. The TV work on the giant side screens was more focused than the whole stage look. Close-ups, winks, visual jokes—Bowie worked hard not to leave one theatrical moment unused. In fact every Bowie show carefully applies rules of theatre to ensure that this diminutive man appears much larger than life.

Of all rockers, Bowie's movement seems most disciplined and least spontaneous. He is an extraordinarily mannered dancer, acting more than dancing. Perhaps the demands of a two-hour live vocal performance require it, but my sense with Bowie is that playing the dancer is simply another role in the vast array of characterizations at his disposal. This approach to performance is not to everyone's liking. I think enjoying a Bowie show is an acquired taste. It's kind of the same as being able to appreciate Liberace, or Tom Jones, or Wayne Newton—they're excessive, but impressive.

We were to get a ride home with the cast of dancers. That meant having to get backstage by the last number. Somehow, with camera, tripod and equipment bag, and the help of Bowie's road manager, we made it backstage in about twenty minutes. We were waiting in a bus as Bowie yelled his final mercis! and bonnes nuits! (What a guy.) He ran offstage and into a Mercedes limo, while our bus immediately filled with sweaty dancers and management. Two minutes later we were on the highway into Paris surrounded by ten motorcycle cops. Other than a very dangerous trip I took once in a Citroen Duex CV over the French Alps with no map, this midnight run stands out as the most incredible vehicular experience I have ever had.

These cops took it on themselves to outperform Bowie. Riding side saddle with legs crossed (at 120 clicks), they cleared traffic ahead of us. They would appear from nowhere and knock on the driver's window, or tap on the hood (still at 120 clicks) and ask him to clear the lane. Once we hit the city, the pace hardly slowed at all. Pedestrians were literally jumping back to the curb to save themselves as we screamed by. When we reached the hotel, the cops were leaning back on their bikes, toothpicks in their mouths. Before any of the punters at the show had left the park, we were back at the hotel showering and making dinner plans.

The next morning Bowie arrived for the interview looking small and tired and immaculate. Clothes look good on him, but it's what is underneath that I find interesting. No real muscle, yet a remarkably strong body. Not really a dancer's form, but the body of a mime artist. Thin through the chest, protruding hip bones and long, expressive arms. No great surprise that he studied with Lindsay Kemp's mime troupe in the 1960s, immediately after leaving a Buddhist monastery in Scotland. He had his own mime company called Feathers, and actually mimed on stage at some T. Rex concerts. It's that training that gives his dancing such a mannered feel—Bowie dances like he has command over the airspace around him.

Anxious as he was to plug the tour, he was also smart enough to acknowledge that he wasn't sure if it was a success. His criteria for the tour this time was to bring everything he knew about theatre to stadium rock. On that level, he had succeeded, but whether or not the rules of theatre that he had applied to the Glass Spider Tour worked in a football stadium was a different matter. Rock shows in football stadiums are basically bad architecture. They tend to dwarf performers instead of making them larger than life. The standard productions shrink the performers even more by using blinding pyrotechnics and oversized set pieces. While Bowie's use of video remains unequalled, the dance was rarely effective as anything more than a kind of Vegas backdrop. While the dancers added energy, there was little point when you couldn't feel or see what they were trying to do.

While the dance style, provided by choreographer Toni Basil, was definitely from the pop world, most of it looked more like antics from the World Wrestling Federation or the latest from the moshing, stage-diving world. The comparisons to Canada's Edouard Locke, of LaLaLa Human Steps, were undeniable. Turns out Bowie had asked Locke to choreograph the show but he had declined, knowing his contribution would never be viewed as anything more than window-dressing. That was a smart move. Bowie came back with another offer—to design the entire "Sound and Vision" show. Using Locke's star dancer, Louise Lecavallier, Locke came out on top, designing a translucent screen seven storeys high on which to project enormous black-and-white images of the dance and Bowie. Meanwhile the stage behind was absolutely bare, making the musicians stand out and seem larger than they were.

What's truly encouraging about Bowie is that he's still capable of experimenting. That's what the Glass Spider Tour was for him, and the fact that it didn't work doesn't seem to have stopped him from continuing to take risks. (After the final show of the tour in New Zealand, Bowie staged a huge party and burned the damned set in a field.) Bowie knows that as soon as he stops taking risks, he's dead, because most of his appeal has come from the fact that this "thin white duke" is able to reinvent himself every time out. Determined to keep up despite his encroaching middle age, he's always a step ahead, even at the risk of seeming unfashionable. Putting all his old songs to rest during the high season for nostalgia, leaving his successful solo career to start a new band (Tin Machine)—whatever you want to say about Bowie, you can't accuse him of being creatively stagnant. He's never been afraid to lose fans.

Bowie "handled" the whole interview. For every question, he was able to give me a decent clip. He knew enough to keep his answers to under a minute and to phrase them in such a way that my questions were not needed. While giving a mildly intelligent answer, he kept his talk simple, not wanting to alienate anyone watching by giving them the impression that he was smarter than they were. All that makes for good TV, but for me, it was infuriating. David Bowie is much more than mildly intelligent—he knows more about painting, theatre and music than most I get to talk to—yet it's only when the cameras are turned off that he will tell you what he's really thinking. It's then that he will answer my questions about the influences of German playwright and lyricist Bertolt Brecht on his work; the distance between stage and audience that Brecht created was an effect that Bowie used for years, while the lyrics Brecht penned in the 1930s sounded timely and new when sung by a baritone rocker like Bowie. It's only when the camera's away that he'll confess his big fascination with Glenn Branca (electric guitar noise wizard), a phase he insists means he's headed in the same direction, away from pop and into the royalty-less world of sound experimentation. But when artists open up only after the cameras are off, it means that they are either extremely nervous or that they are manipulating the entire procedure to achieve their own ends. In Bowie's case, it was both. Worse than any politician, he's constantly thinking beyond the moment, the question and the technology. He's got his one blue eye on the image that will finally be beamed into your living room, and if he wants to be sure he's projecting his image du jour, he can't afford to engage in real conversation. After all these years, I don't think Bowie has the nerve to be himself on TV.

Two months later Bowie brought his Glass Spider Tour to Toronto and I interviewed him again, live on Much. The ultimate professional, he remembered our Paris interview, my name and everything we talked about. He invited me backstage to see him before the show.

Arriving at the trailer marked "Management Office" I introduced myself and was led to Bowie's trailer. Backstage at the CNE was crazy with activity. As the exhaustion of the two-day load-in procedure was beginning to show, the pre-gig excitement was kicking in. Dozens of assistant types, in leggings and fancy running shoes, with every conceivable laminate around their neck, were running to the press entrance with special passes, faxes, photo and TV waivers. Union representatives were cranky after dealing with the elaborate requests for the Glass Spider set and had to be handled diplomatically. The craft service had just finished serving dinner to the crew and were gearing up again to have another meal ready for after the show. Big, beefy local security gangs were being briefed by one of the assistants about what was going to happen in the show, and about four dozen people standing around doing nothing but lapping up the excitement of the event and the free beer in the hospitality tent looked conspicuously out of place. They were the usual suspects, overweight DJs, record company receptionists and contest winners, feeling hopeful that some of Bowie's talent and fame was rubbing off on them.

Bowie was sitting by himself watching multicultural TV in his trailer. We sat and talked as his assistant hovered close by. It was nice not to talk about music. We talked about books, eating, dancing and multicultural TV. It was nice to see that Bowie prepared for his show in the same way an actor or a dancer would—warm-up exercises, quiet concentration, TV on in the background. The hangers-on in the hospitality suite would have been devastated. It was impressive to think that all the activity outside this trailer was because of one man's talent. While this level of organization comes with any major star, Bowie treats his talent and his performance very seriously. He feels a great responsibility to his fans and to himself to do his best work, and his crew seemed to have the same work ethic.

After about fifteen minutes I left to let him contemplate his long climb up to the suspended Glass Spider while I contemplated our untelevised chat. It struck me that it was the first time I'd felt he was truly answering my questions—the first time we'd really had a conversation. He comes by his moniker "the chameleon of rock" honestly. He has a disguise for every situation, and a motive for every move. Bowie still can't come clean after twenty-five years.

## annie lennox

At the beginning of their career, the Eurythmics did interviews together, but somewhere along the line Annie Lennox put her foot down: she didn't like them and she didn't want to do them any more. It wasn't until *We Two Are One* came out in 1989 that I got to meet her.

Their international record release was held in Juan les Pins, on the Mediterranean, just outside Antibes, France. After travelling to London, I got on a chartered jet full of bitter English journalists who were working up a scam to play on the front desk clerk at our hotel in Cannes to get room upgrades. They were noisy, drunk and had already made bets on who would ask the tactless question about the baby Annie had lost in childbirth. An entirely unlikeable lot that were to be avoided at all costs, I left them to their sweaty, cynical selves for the next two days.

The Eurythmics were going to perform on the beach at Juan les Pins, and it would be a full production—the first look at their upcoming tour. The locals were invited, and the show was a blast. Standing with my feet in the sand with a thousand others, watching the band perform their new and old material, was a quality job perk for me. It was worth the jet lag to end up knee-deep in the Mediterranean watching the fireworks that finished a remarkable show. Afterwards, they threw a major party on the beach with fabulous food, music and pretty French boys. (The English journalists were huddled in a corner complaining about the heat.) A great way to tear down a journalist's resistance you would think, but all the pampering serves as a constant reminder that they are attempting to soothe you into a favourable state of mind, and so your resolve to hold on to some objectivity simply gets stronger.

The next morning we were to attend a press conference, where the print journalists would ask their questions. Afterwards, we were to have our TV interview. Rather than a regular press conference, Dave and Annie had planned to do acoustic versions of some of the new material on the album. Waiting for them to show up, I noticed a hotel employee bring in a lectern with a microphone on it. He unscrewed the microphone from the stand, plugged it in to a loud-speaker sound system that was permanently installed in the room for business meeting purposes and gave it the old "*Allo, Allo*" routine. The feedback made the room momentarily go silent. I guess he thought feedback meant it was working properly, since he set the microphone down on the table and left.

Dave and Annie arrived and started into their musical press conference, Dave on guitar and Annie on the impossible microphone meant only for speeches about marketing initiatives from French businessmen. She struggled gamely with the bashed-up mike from what looked like the 1960s. Fortunately, part of a good singer's talent is compensating for technology. Mike technique means a lot more than whether you hold it or put it in a stand. You shape your voice differently for different microphones; you have to be able to adjust your volume, your distance from the mike and the tone of your voice to make up for a microphone's inadequacies. That Annie did, but barely.

Singing over, she took the first question. She happened to get the hungover English journalist who immediately asked her what it was like to lose a baby during birth. She mumbled something to the effect that it shouldn't be too difficult to understand how traumatic it is, and that her feelings were too personal for her to talk about. Dave took over. He handled the musical questions with ease and humour, and I could tell he was trying to soothe Annie at the same time. But the room, not having had a chance to talk to Annie in years, kept zeroing in on her and her politics. Since she's a well-known strict vegetarian, they wondered if she, like Chrissie Hynde, advocated bombing McDonalds. Given that she had done a video for Greenpeace, how come she was staying in a hotel that didn't recycle and had white toilet paper? How did she get her body back in shape after the baby, and when would she be having another "go" at the baby thing. No wonder she despises the media. At every one of these questions I became more and more embarrassed for her, and for myself, being lumped in with the rest of these journalists.

The press conference was over and we were set up outdoors for the interview. Annie arrived livid, partly because of the treatment she was subjected to at the hands of the press, but mostly because of the ridiculous sound system she had had to deal with. She was screaming at her manager (and I thought rightly so), wondering why their soundman, who was on full-time salary, hadn't been brought in to oversee the sound. She wanted to know who made the sound arrangements. The manager apologized up and down, saying the hotel had assured him the sound would be fine. Annie's reply was, "Since when do hotel managers know anything about sound?" He shut up and scuttled out of the room so we could have our interview.

"So this is the big time," I said. Impossible to imagine that a group of their stature couldn't manage to find people to take care of the littlest thing like one good microphone. They both agreed: it doesn't matter how big you get, how much money you make, or pay, everything still rests on the artists' shoulders. Annie said the acoustic press conference was the one detail she hadn't checked in the whole weekend's extravaganza, and, sure enough, it had screwed up. Not only had it sounded bad, but the TV cameras there had not been able to film it, because no accommodation had been made for them to plug in a line feed. What's the point of a press conference that can't be taped?

Listening to the two of them talk before we started rolling, it became apparent just how their collaboration worked. Annie is all passion and inspiration; Dave Stewart is calm and easygoing, setting a relaxed mood for Annie. They go into the studio every time with no preconceived songs, so each record presents a huge amount of risk for them. Will they be able to work with each other? Will their imaginations dry up? While Annie works very hard on language—she never wants to waste a word—some of her best lines are improvised.

Dave just keeps the tape rolling while Annie flies off in all directions. They say working together is not a pleasant experience at all. While Annie is very critical, Dave is much less so; Annie holds Dave back, and he pushes her forward. She frequently wants to give up; he won't let her. It's so intense that people around them can't watch. A soul-baring time for Annie, she exposes herself to the point of emotional exhaustion. After the record is completed, instead of promoting it, she would rather bury it.

But all this angst makes good music. The best songwriting duos in rock history are built around friction and pressure. Lennon and McCartney, Richards and Jagger wrote under the same kinds of difficult working conditions. For the Eurythmics, it has paid off with some songs that are able to encompass more than the usual limited emotional vocabulary. Songs full of melancholy, wit, parody and compassion have consistently managed to hit the top ten. A great Eurythmics song is like having someone to touch you, but they are able to go right through skin to the bone. That's great writing.

## mick jagger

Mick Jagger put out *Let's Work* in 1987, and MuchMusic was told if we could get ourselves to Paris we could have an interview. It was unusual for Much to actually pay for any trip, but Mick Jagger hadn't been "done" yet, so they succumbed. When they found out that the airfare would be cheaper if I stayed for eight days instead of the three I would need to do the job, they went for the extended trip. (If they had only added up the extra hotel days and meals they would have figured out that it was far more expensive, but they didn't, and I didn't tell them.) I got eight days in Paris in October with nothing to do but research, which I found could best be done sitting in an outdoor café by the Luxembourg Gardens.

My evenings were taken care of. Basil, my cameraman, had never been to France, hated wine and nouvelle cuisine, so I took it on myself to force him to enjoy all of these things. (I wasn't very successful with the wine; he mixes it with ginger ale to this day.) Also, two friends of mine had recently moved to Paris to work, he to draw and she to model. After a particularly torturous evening with Basil in a restaurant (Basil would burst out laughing at the piddling portion on his plate when the waiter presented him with his meal), we would head to Bernie and Dionne's apartment for more food and wine.

Basil spent his days at the museums and shops—not buying, just pricing things. I have never met anyone who knows what a bargain is better than Basil. (Conversely, when I'm on a trip and I see something I like, I buy it on the spot. I don't care how much it is. To be able to say I bought this shirt in Paris, the jacket in Hamburg and the pants at Zeller's is worth any price.) My days were spent reading, and there is far too much to read about the Stones. After six days I couldn't take it any more. Every biography I read covered the same well-known facts, with little or no insight or criticism. I lost any perspective that I once had myself. I ditched the books, ordered some more warm goat cheese on toast to go with my wine and started to listen on my Walkman. The Stones material left me reeling by its sheer volume, but Jagger's solo work was ripe with questions. Why was he singing country? Was it parody, or was he really going for it? And what about *Let's Work*. Was he serious? Since when has the work ethic been high on the Stones' list of lyrical themes? About the working class, yes, but "Let's get down to it and get a job"?

My big interest in Jagger (as far as the Stones years went) was how they started, sitting on stools, playing in a very subdued traditional blues style—and how they ended up, being one of the most physical and interesting stage bands in rock history. Where did those movements come from? When one thinks of Jagger, his movement is probably half of what you know about him. Almost more important than the music, the way he moves is a better definition for rock and roll than anything else. (The same can be said for Elvis Presley, infamous for his movement just as much as his music.)

The night before the interview I worked out my ideas on my friends after dinner. It must have been a terrible bore (none of them being Stones fans) but very helpful to me to actually say out loud what I had been coming up with in my head all week. It was arranged that Bernie would accompany Basil and me to the George V hotel in the morning to take some publicity stills.

The typical round robin of interviews was happening. Two suites were occupied; while one crew was shooting their interview, another crew in the other suite was setting up. This was the only press for *Let's Work* Jagger was going to do, so just about every country seemed to have an interview slot.

As we were setting up, Jagger's manager appeared and wanted to know what I was going to talk to Jagger about. He wanted to relay that information to Jagger so Mick would not be totally surprised. (I can't imagine Jagger being flustered in an interview. He's done more of them than anyone else in the business.) The manager was surprised when I mentioned the movement angle and left to tell Jagger.

We were set, Mick arrived, and I must admit I was immediately struck by his size—he's tiny. And for all the creases on his face, he's eternally young. He has the smile of a six-year-old, and a bad six-year-old at that. He was friendly, but guarded. I could tell he was not going to give away one hint of his true self in this interview, or any other. After forty minutes with Jagger, I didn't have any more of a clue about what Mick Jagger was like than before I met him. There is an ocean of oblivion between what Jagger does for a living, and who he really is. Supposedly, he's had an autobiography due to come out for years now. Why it hasn't been published has been greatly speculated about—Jagger's really such a boring fellow the book is just too banal, or his soul is too dark to ever be exposed, or Mick is incapable of telling the truth about himself. I like to think it's because he understands that his mystique is far more powerful than anything he could ever say about himself.

What he did tell me is that the most important thing about his music is that it makes people dance. And to do that, he has to want to dance to it too. It wasn't always that way. In the beginning, the Stones wanted to be a serious blues band—part of a hip, underground scene happening in London. But after he and Richards starting writing together, the music changed and the sit-down approach to the music had to go. While everyone else in the band had an instrument in front of him, Jagger felt very exposed. He couldn't simply stand there, he had to move. He copied no one, he simply made it up as he went along. He sees his movement as a pure expression of the music. So much so that to this day, most of the communication done in the studio to clue in other musicians is done through dance. He danced the sax solo for Sonny Rollins to play on "Tattoo You."

Jagger judges the success of his songwriting by what it makes his feet do. Not exactly a thinking man's approach to rock and roll but an honest, instinctual one that can't be faked. Even so, I still contend that Jagger is a very bright fellow who hides behind dark glasses. Even through the drug-crazed years of the 1970s, Jagger managed to stay totally in tune with the times. *Exile On Main Street* says more about that decade than any other album, his political turn on *Undercover* was timely without jumping on the political bandwagon that many other bands were diving for, and his ability to keep coming out fresh and not letting his past freeze him out of a future takes brains.

## bryan ferry

Okay, so I'm a Bryan Ferry freak. Ever since Roxy Music's first album in 1972, I have been hooked. Never had a voice like that been heard in rock and roll, and never had their quirky mix of 1950s cheesecake and futuristic glam been tried before. It worked better visually than it did musically at the beginning, I think. The production of the early Roxy albums is awfully cluttered. Using the piano as a key element of the band's sound, along with woodwinds and Eno's Moog, made for busy records. On stage, they were a soundman's nightmare, using pre-recorded tape loops that needed split-second accuracy. On first listen, they could have been described as a campy King Crimson, but by the time *For Your Pleasure*, the second Roxy album, came out in 1973, they had established themselves as one of the most original and influential bands around.

The trick with Roxy Music was figuring out where Ferry was coming from. The tips of the hat to the worlds of art, literature and fashion, and to the musical past, were everywhere in his work. Ferry takes his lyrical style from the world of pop art. Throwaway clichés and idioms of the day are carefully juxtaposed to create a language that sounds more exotic than any of its elements. All of his song titles sound like they've come from magazines—"In Every Dream Home A Heartache," "The Right Stuff," "Flesh and Blood," "Sign of the Times." He usually scat-sings his songs first to find out what sounds work best where, then replaces those vowels or consonants with bits of found language. When asked for his influences, Ferry hardly ever cites other musicians. Instead, he looks to the literature of T.S. Eliot and F. Scott Fitzgerald, or artists Marcel Duchamp and Andy Warhol. Music is a visual thing to Ferry, a total pop-art concept expressed in music. Before he had even formed the band he had the name, knew how they would dress, the look of their posters and the era they would epitomize.

I met Ferry in New York just before Christmas in 1988. He had just released *Bête Noire* and was in New York rehearsing for "Saturday Night Live." We set up in the Warner Brothers offices and waited for his rehearsal at NBC to end so our interview could begin. I was truly anxious—worried that I would be disappointed after all these years of thinking Bryan Ferry was the best thing since Adam, and worried that he wasn't going to ask me to run away with him at the conclusion of the interview. I also should have been worried that my questions were too "inside" for the regular viewer—interviews done by fans tend to be exceedingly boring for anyone not as obsessed by the band as the interviewer is—but I couldn't have cared less. I had forty minutes of time with my hero of fifteen years, and I wasn't going to let anything like professionalism stop me from getting what I wanted out of this interview.

By the time he showed up, two hours late, I was a bag of nerves. When I get nervous, I get very sleepy, so when he arrived I was sleeping on the couch. Not quite the first impression I had wanted to leave, but there it was. We opened two beers and settled in to talk. The cameraman told Bryan his tie was a little off-centre, and he replied, "Yes, I wear them that way." Ferry has to remake and remodel every little thing.

What I wanted to know was what made him switch from a career as a painter to one as an art rocker. For all the influences he had absorbed from the world of art, there had to be a major musical one that made him turn to music. After his High Road Tour of 1983, I'd decided that I had figured out what that musical influence was. With its immense band, three back-up vocalists and a tuxedoed Ferry in front, it looked just like the famous Stax Volt Revue of 1967. Otis Redding was on that bill, and the show was a powerhouse of Memphis soul. I asked Ferry if he had seen that show. He had, and said it was the best thing he's ever seen. He had hitched in to London and the Roundhouse to see the show, and what he had seen and heard on stage that night appealed to him as the complete art package—far more potent and physical than the art world could offer. Ferry decided he wanted a piece of it. After that I wasn't nervous any more. The fear of interviewing your idol is that you'll find out you have been completely on the wrong wavelength for years. Hitting the Stax Volt influence assured me that I had been on the right track, and at that moment I knew the rest of the interview would fall into place.

Ferry is one artist whose image is more accessible than his music. Classic good looks combined with classic clothes make the man. He has never been averse to using himself as a canvas, both to add to the total concept of the band and to sell the music. From the very beginnings of Roxy Music, Ferry found himself photographed all the time, and he quickly decided to use that fact to his advantage. He likes the look of men's uniforms, so he tried just about every one imaginable, from suit and tie (when it was highly unfashionable in the mid-1970s), to black-hatted Valentino, fascist khakis to smoking jacket to white T-shirt. But none of these stuck like the image of Ferry in a white dinner jacket and black tux pants. He had no idea it would be so potent and can only attribute it to the combination of two such unlike things—traditional formal wear and rock and roll on the same stage. An image he would have liked to drop, it has stuck with him for almost nineteen years now.

Somewhere along the line Ferry lost his delight in using his image to help make the music go. He would much rather sit in a studio now and make records (let someone else hand them out) and get on with more music. The thought of talking about a finished product or extensively touring an album of songs he considers completed holds no excitement for him any more. If anything, he finds repolishing his image a distraction. Bryan Ferry has completely changed his tune; all he desires now is complete privacy to do his work. Unlike so many other "art rockers" who in their forties find out that their music isn't enough to satisfy their artistic needs, Ferry is totally satisfied by the music and is letting the visual and image end of his career relax. At the same time, the music is getting more and more subtle—more mood music than rock. He still uses the pop art idea of taking his lyrics from everyday usage, but he has other things to say now. "Dance away the heartache" and "Love is the drug" are lines from a different era, and to write about more mature ideas, still using the language and musical backbone of the youth culture, is the new challenge for Ferry. That's why his albums now take forever to finish. As his style moves beyond the parameters of rock, Ferry is loathe to give up the beat. I wonder how long the struggle to marry the two will continue. When will Ferry cross over to the other side and give us something totally outside the world of rock that he has influenced so much in the last twenty years?

For the record, Ferry didn't ask me to run away with him, but I got over it. Just to know that my interpretation of his work pretty much hit the nail on the head was reward enough. Almost.

For every one of these interviews with thinking musicians, or the "naturals," with talent oozing out of every pore, I did seventy-five with bands of no real ability whatsoever—musicians with no idea what their music was about, poseurs who were dressing up and regurgitating their best imitation of the top ten. My favourite opening question to that kind of band is "What makes you think you're any different from any other band that comes through here?" The look of fear that crosses their faces is small consolation for having to eke out a couple of good clips to build a story around.

It's the thousands of these bands that give rock and roll a bad name. They are so concerned with appropriate accessories and convincing details that assure them membership in the rock world that it becomes easy to believe that rock is a very limited form, with only so many chord possibilities and lyrical themes. These poseurs have set a strict form for themselves to follow; they want their stuff to fall well within the boundaries of mainstream pop and rock. What they've done, in their search for success, is breed a generation of rock fans who now distrust anything that falls outside this norm. If it doesn't sound like recycled drivel, it's suspect. While rock was once the arena where anything goes, it is now too often a very narrow-minded beast.

The poseur is the one who welcomes the music industry into the studio, who thinks the guys in suits know more about music than they do. How different from the real innovators in rock. Joe Jackson describes the music industry as a pool of alligators between him and his audience; His job is to somehow cross the pool without turning into an alligator himself. The poseurs, on the other hand, think the alligators are their key to success. They want millions to hear their music, not because they think what they have to say is particularly relevant, but because it will ensure mega royalty checks.

Perhaps the easiest way to spot a poseur is to look for "rock face." Just as their music reflects what they think you want to hear, the way they look reflects the way they think rock stars are supposed to look. The mouth is eternally open, either pouting (main activity of singer when not singing) or the biting-lip grimace (main activity of guitar poseur). Contrary to what they would have you believe, not all musicians are mouth-breathers.

Maybe I'm being a little too hard on the poor old rock world, but what I think or write about it isn't going to affect it one tiny bit. The beautiful thing about popular music is that everyone's opinion is as valid as mine. You don't need to be on the inside to decide whether you're listening to a real talent or not. In my job as music journalist, I may be one of the first people to give you an opinion about a band's talent, but music critics in North America never have the last word. You do.

# the box rocks

in which television triumphs over rock, to our general dismay

I've come to understand what William Blake meant when he said that children are born complete and the process of "civilizing" them means that completeness is chipped away and replaced with a pared-down level of experience that their parents and other adults can understand and deal with. The pleasure my one-year-old daughter Hadley got out of watching and hearing the opening credits to "The Flintstones" every day came from the pure delight of being bombarded with meaningless sight and sound. She was not passive; she reacted. She got up and danced around the room and sang along. It's sensory stimulation, not deprivation, probably only available to a one-year-old. And it's at that level that TV is probably best enjoyed.

It's my view that in the space of a generation, and for some reason I can't pretend to understand (it may have to do with the electromagnetic radiation emanating from the screen), the human genetic code seems to have been altered to the point that we are born with an ability to watch TV. Take the aforementioned Hadley, for instance, who, at the age of thirteen months, could take the remote in her tiny fingers and manipulate the power switch, change the volume and run through the channels until she found something she liked.

Nobody taught Haddie how to watch TV, but she adores it. Maybe she heard so much of it in the womb as I sat doing all-night edits that it became a pre-conscious phenomenon. I assume that it's the colours and the fast changes of light and dark that captivate her. I never even notice them until I'm driving through a neighbourhood at night, seeing through the windows all the flickering blue light reflected off the inside walls and ceilings.

The way we "read" TV is changing. As TV sinks further into the popular consciousness, future generations will use and react to TV differently. My generation was the first to grow up with TV. By the time I had memory (aged three) all houses in my experience had TVs, soon to be colour, and soon more than one. But it was still a foreign, mysterious, veneered box in the corner—no one I knew was *on* TV. (The fact that I actually received a postcard from "Chez Helene" totally confounded me. I had no idea that she truly existed in this world.) For Hadley, it will be quite different. Hers will be the first generation to actually have grown up on TV. She can see herself on TV anytime, courtesy of the video-8 camera. She can also see her mother on TV, and often does, and from a very early age she knew who it was. Frequently, on early morning studio gigs for "Midday," Haddie would sit in the control room watching me on the TV monitor telling her to sit still and be quiet because we were about to roll tape. It worked. Some TV paranoids will shudder at that and pronounce Haddie another TV victim, but TV will be utterly demystified for her. She will make TV in school, she will take courses on TV, she and her friends will play games on it, and soon it will be genuinely interactive. The approach these kids bring to TV will make it utterly different from the semi-religious star vehicle it has been in the past, and TV will likely play an even more central role in their lives than it has so far in ours.

So what is this thing that demands so much and gives so little? How would you describe TV to the uninitiated? Marshall McLuhan says James Joyce called TV, then in its very early days, the "Charge of the Light Brigade" that imbues his "soulskin with subconscious inklings." Says McLuhan: "The TV image is not a still shot. It is not a photo in any sense, but a ceaselessly-forming contour of things lined by the scanning finger. The resulting plastic contour is lit from within so the image formed has the quality of sculpture, rather than a picture. While that sculpture offers some three million dots per second to the receiver, he accepts only a few dozen each instant, from which to make an image."* That's what all the fuss is about. (I have as

*Marshall McLuhan, *Understanding Media* (New York: Mentor Books, 1964).

much trouble with that as I do with the fact that glass is not a solid but a liquid!) My favourite description of the "wired world" comes from Stewart Brand at the Massachusetts Intitute of Technology's "Media Lab." He concludes: "The wired world is a teenager with a new car, taking dumb risks, finding new freedoms. It's a privilege to be around self-discovery like that, but gruelling, and sometimes tragic."

Well, that sounds to me like a dead-on definition of rock and roll!

## in the beginning

Rock and roll and TV are essentially fraternal in that both were popularized about the same time—in the Eisenhower "Father Knows Best" heyday after World War II. Both have their roots in popular culture—the earliest TV was simply putting pictures to radio shows, and rock and roll was indebted to the blues and jazz of the 1930s. In fact, their family tree mingles in the pre-war era since many of the truly successful radio shows were in fact music shows, and that music tended to be big band jazz, which itself was, by lineage, black (although no one would admit it at the time) and blues-inspired.

Music did not transfer particularly well to TV, being inherently non-visual. And the state of the technology didn't help; the speakers in TVs cost less than 1 percent of the total price of the machine. My guess is that's why radio variety shows, which were mainly musical, became, when transferred to TV, largely comedy skits, which played better over bad speakers, and which in turn begat the dreaded TV sitcom.

Pop music stayed on radio. Big band jazz turned out to be a surprisingly limited form and tended to disappear as its proponents and fans aged. Technology advanced; musicians could make the same big noise as a big band with a lot fewer players through the use of amplifiers and electric instruments.

Meanwhile the post-war industrial expansion required a vast, low-paid labour force. As black Americans began their earnest trudge towards the American dream, their blues, soul and gospel music preceded them onto Main Street America and was eagerly appropriated by working-class whites. Why this happened has been recounted countless times in various Elvis bios. My main point is that while middle-class America tuned into the "General Electric Hour," hosted by Ronald Reagan, on their General Electric TVs, lower-class Americans, black and white, and rural Canadians stayed tuned into the radio, where programming was often more liberal because it was not necessary to specify the race of the invisible artists. By the time the music had enough currency to demand that it be seen, there were enough white artists doing it that it could move to TV and film. The uncredited and unpaid black artists remained behind in the big dance halls and theatres like the Apollo in New York.

I don't know when rock and roll first made it to TV. Probably in some newsreel filler footage of white boys gyrating to black music, or some pseudo-news feature of teenaged girls showing their underwear while jitterbugging to some jazz crossover like Cab Calloway.

Certainly Elvis made it to TV, but far more often, I think, in news clips and for having his ears exposed during army inductions. "Scopitones," a television jukebox located in some bars and diners in the States, were the first to offer us pictures of mostly unknown pop wannabes lip-synching to popular songs—no band, no evidence of music being made, just corny choreography and big-chested women.

Like everybody else, I first saw rock and roll on TV in the comfort of my parent's rec room, on Ed Sullivan. Those clips have been replayed so often that I honestly can't remember if I saw them when they first aired or only later in films. The one I did see was the "She Loves You" Beatles presentation; it was absolutely apparent to me that this was something powerful and influential and attractive and important. Kids in my school collected Beatles photos on bubble-gum cards. And here they were on the pinnacle of achievement, Ed Sullivan! Everything that I felt about that was obviously felt by millions—and by director Richard Lester, who took that feeling and made it into the Beatles' first film, *A Hard Day's Night*.

*A Hard Day's Night* was made as a quickie exploitation movie to rob me of my two-dollar allowance in 1965. I was eight; the Beatles were in their early twenties. A big part of the fascination of *A Hard Day's Night* was that it provided us with an introduction to rock technology. A lot of Lester's camera work in the film focuses on how rock music gets made: how Lennon approaches the microphone; how that Harrison riff gets made on the guitar; Ringo's rim-shots. More important, it was also about how rock on TV gets made, and the effect of rock on TV and vice versa. The central story shows the band's tribulations in getting to a TV studio for a Sullivan-like spot. You can see the band through the TV camera viewfinder and watch the director cutting the live shots together.

What made this low-budget exploitation film seem counter-culture was its conveyance of an attitude about being on TV. Some foolish Vegas-style dance routine set against giant photos of bugs (beetles) to a swing version of "Happy Just to Dance with You" is being rehearsed as an introductory piece before the band's appearance. In that, the difference—musically and stylistically—between rock and roll and TV is made very plain. TV tones things down, remakes them into smarmy, uninteresting pablum, doesn't get it, isn't hip and can't possibly hope to tune into what really matters. Not coincidentally, in another room in the studio, advertisers are getting ready to launch a line of "hip" clothing. When George wanders into the room by mistake, he is interviewed as a one-person focus group by the ad execs, and he tells them that their promo girl is a "well-known drag" and that he and his mates sit around and watch her on the telly and have "a right good giggle." *A Hard Day's Night* made what rock-and-rollers thought about TV very clear. (I have also noticed that the film is not often shown on TV, maybe because it cuts too close to the bone.)

When Don Kirshner attempted to rip off *A Hard Day's Night* in 1966 with TV's "The Monkees," what he tried to put into a weekly series was the kind of infectious smart-assedness that Lennon showed in *A Hard Day's Night.* Of course the music was pathetic; it had no genuine rock resonance, and the made-for-TV band, by definition, had nothing to do with what rock was all about. But its major failure was in missing a sense of "group," the sense of us-against-them, the sense of "isn't this a major giggle?" the absolute self-confidence in language and style and fashion and sensibility. Now, like any ten-year-old, I was won over and easily manipulated by the Monkees, through constant exposure in teen magazines, on the radio and on TV. And by the time I was cluing into the fact, the Beatles had stopped performing live, made a dreadful movie called *Help* and were putting out peculiar concept albums that were above my head called things like *Sgt. Pepper* and *Magical Mystery Tour.*

For most of the 1960s and 1970s, rock and roll essentially stayed on radio. When it did venture into the world of TV, it was in the form of band guest spots on variety shows. Even unusually progressive shows, such as "The Smothers Brothers," tended to shoot quite static performances of bands with wide appeal lip-synching to their hit records. Even when the quality of the music was acceptable (although drastically thinned out for the minuscule television speaker), the quality of the lip-synching was not. In the early days, no one practised lip-synching—not many rock-and-rollers would put that much effort into TV. Twenty-five years later, Milli Vanilli would prove in the era of rock videos that lip-synching is the only talent you need to get an audience. Because of that rather embarrassing fact, and pressure from musicians, who are in demand for TV, the rules have been changed. Performers now show up to TV studios with cassette tapes of the music for their hit songs that do not have the vocals included in the mix, and the vocals are sung live during the TV performance. At least this way something musical actually happens during the TV taping.

My favourite story of the pioneers of rock TV comes from England in the early 1960s. The BBC had a completely dead hour of air at the start of prime time, which was designated "the Quiet Hour," the hour of no TV, the hour to put the children to bed. (They knew enough about TV even then to realize that it's almost impossible to pull children out of a room with a TV on.) In a daring move, a renegade BBC producer suggested that they try a live rock show in their only open time slot, the Quiet Hour. Funnily enough, the toughest thing to get past management was the idea that the show's live audience would not be sitting but standing, as though they were at a rock or dance club. They would dance, not attend a concert. It was a risky move, one that took a lot of control away from the TV people and gave it to the performers and the audience. For the first time, cameras and lights would have to work around the action instead of dictating it. But the BBC was in desperate need of programming that appealed to a teenage audience, so *Top of the Pops* was born. TV took its first baby-step towards rock and roll.

The limited appeal of rock on TV is due as much to the failure of TV directors to understand the music as it is to any of TV's technological limitations. TV directors tend not to be rock and roll aficionados, or they wouldn't shoot it the way they do. Putting rock and roll on TV demands complete compromise on the part of the musicians. In the 1970s, rock bands on TV looked like anything but. Set designers and directors moved band members around like furniture, trying to find new and eye-pleasing ways of presenting these cumbersome instruments. In reality, you can never have a bass player more than ten feet away from the drummer, and eye contact between the two is essential—but for TV the drummer would find himself on a shaky eight-foot riser made to look like a military bass drum, not hearing or seeing any of his mates, and feeling like a fool. Mick Jagger would be told he could only move about two feet to either side—otherwise he would be out of his light. Forget about playing to the live audience that has lined up for ten hours outside to see this taping—play right for the cameras. Usually there were three cameras, and the only way the musicians could tell which camera was "on" was by checking to see which one had its red light lit up. So the band tried to give a performance without hearing the music, trying to ignore the raging hormones in the audience, and kept their eyes trained to the tops of the cameras where the frigging red lights were. Pavlov's dog could have shown them a thing or two.

TV was (and to a great extent still is) so self-absorbed and self-inflated that it didn't even dawn on the producers that they were asking the band to make a compromise. So the sulky and uncooperative musicians they pushed around became the awful people that TV associated with "that awful music." If it wasn't for the fabulous ratings these shows got, TV would have canned the whole idea.

Not a lot has changed. In 1984, my band, The Crowd in History, was on a CBC TV show that was a battle-of-the-bands kind of thing. (I remember Alannah Myles entered too. We both made it to the semifinals.) The director (who kept yelling "Bongo! Bongo!" when things went right, reminding me of the director in *A Hard Day's Night*) concentrated on shooting the singers. Since I was one of them, that was all right with me, but he essentially ignored everyone else, despite the fact that we had some interesting instrumentation (a female fiddler and a very hot guitarist) and that the whole sense of the song was in a very intricate and complicated drum rhythm. The result—with a lot of dry ice swirling around and swooping crane shots—was ridiculous. At least the song had to be performed live, it being a contest of sorts.

Not until the show went to air, and our band was sweating around our TV set, did we discover that the producers had cut two verses and a chorus out of our live performance. We were incensed! Never had there been any indication from the producers that the song was too long and we should regig it for them. For those band members that worked in TV, it was no big deal. For those in the band who were musicians first, it was a case of misrepresentation, bowdlerization and creative insult. The show's producer justified it by saying that we were the winners of that week's show so they thought we wouldn't mind them cutting the song. That attitude is the polar opposite to a musician's—in TV, creative intent, performance and respect for the music come way down the list.

## strange bedfellows

Luckily for everyone, rock has always had a life apart from radio and TV. You could make rock and roll yourself. Go ahead and try this at home, kids, in your basement or garage. Get your parents to shell out for that Sears six-string plunker or drum kit. Get the other kids to do the same. Put your latest 45 on the player, grab the vacuum hose and lip-synch someplace where you won't be too embarrassed if your mom comes downstairs unexpectedly. Grow your hair—it's your hair, after all, and nobody else's, so why can't you do it the way you like? Tell your parents you're going to Janie's pyjama party up the street and then sneak off to Buffalo for the Bowie concert. Rock and roll—both as a musical form and as a lifestyle—has always been available and do-able in the comfort of your own life. Not so with TV. TV was Disney animal shows, Rob Petrie and his older coworkers at the office, "My Mother the Car."

TV is about other things. It captures its natural subject matter well enough, and after infusing it with all sorts of standards, limits and restriction spits it back out. It is only rarely that TV is original, in and of itself. It can bring you a concert, but that concert, not the broadcast on TV, is the original. It can bring you a news report, but the news event itself is the original, not the report of it.

You can tell this is true, because the best TV is

about one thing only—TV. By the early 1960s, TV had a ten-year grip on the middle-class mind that was as powerful as the pull to panel the rec room, and the extended, self-referential parody could begin. Perhaps the first parody was "The Dick Van Dyke Show" (about a TV comedy show writer). By the 1970s television had fully realized two things. It was the most potent cultural force around, and it had nothing to say. Consequently the best TV shows in the 1970s and 1980s were cannabalizing TV: "Saturday Night Live," with the "Not Ready for Prime Time Players" and their spoofs of TV sitcoms and news, and Second City's "SCTV," which built its whole show around the one-joke premise of a small TV station (often thought to have been modelled broadly on Citytv in Toronto, although David Cronenberg already captured City in his film *Videodrome*). Even "The Mary Tyler Moore Show" was about TV news. Today, three programs represent the best of TV: the cartoon series "The Simpsons," which is parodic of everything from "The Jetsons" and "The Flintstones" to "The Cosby Show"; "Seinfeld," the show about nothing, where the characters try to create their own TV sitcom about exactly that; and "The Gary Shandling Show," the behind-the-scenes TV talk show from hell.

To me, TV programs that are not about TV rarely seem to last, because they are lost in the noise and the wash. Only when TV talks about itself does it seem to be valid; it startles us because it is a reflection of a reflection, like the use of mirrors in some art movie or the lady with the Dutch Cleanser can on the label of a can of Dutch Cleanser. However, this kind of satire is art of a second order, because the only original thing about it is the technology and technique of the form itself. The content is hollow; the emperor has no clothes.

This is not simply the old argument that satire is a lower form of art than the truly original stuff. Lampooning through quotes and references can be great, fun stuff. Satire also assists media literacy: watching the Ted Baxter character on "The Mary Tyler Moore Show" massacre the news is a good, popular lesson about the distortions of TV journalism. It's simply that TV is, as author Joyce Nelson has called it, the "perfect machine" to illustrate how the medium itself is the only message it can effectively carry. It would be like endlessly looking through a telescope and seeing only an image of a telescope. The only thing original about the content of TV is the fact that it is being presented on TV; and the only good thing on TV is satire of TV; and as somebody once said, "satire is the last flicker of originality."

On the other hand, rock and roll is undeniably and wholly an original, or at least it was until it began to be appropriated by TV. If the ideology of TV is capitalism, the ideology of rock and roll is revolution. So, as rock and roll grabbed more and more of our spending money and began hitting the news as well as the charts, rock and roll became a very obvious target for TV.

## the citytv experiment

In my opinion, and in my experience, rock and roll only began to successfully make it to TV in North

America with the advent of Citytv in Toronto, in the early 1970s. This was a local TV station with a rock and roll attitude. As a non-union workplace, it tended to attract young people right out of radio and television arts colleges, some of whom would work for free just to get the experience. City was irreverent and hip in its programming. It blatantly used sex (its regular "baby blue" soft porn movies) to build an audience. It showed rock and roll movies on weekends, as well as both cult and truly bad films. It had dance-party shows and showcase shows for young performers. By the late 1970s it had hired a director of music programming. Even before the advent of music videos, it developed a program called "The NewMusic" to talk to rock musicians and shoot their live performances. That meant, for the first time in North American television, TV was going to the rock and roll club, to see rock in its environment, instead of deflating rock and roll by insisting that it come under the hot scrutiny of the TV studio lights. And in that simple manoeuvre, rock and roll could (almost successfully) be seen (if not very well heard) on television for the first time.

Working around the musicians' schedules meant that interviews usually happened after the show, at about 1:00 a.m. Rock clubs weren't usually very generous with the stage lights, so most of the footage was dark red and blurry. The soundman didn't have any idea what kind of sound requirements TV needed, so more often than not the sound was not that great. And the audience weren't exactly thrilled to see TV trying to invade their ultra-cool lifestyle.

I didn't envy those early rock journalists. J.D. Roberts, Jeanne Beker and Daniel Richler were brave souls, for not only was the audience unkind, the musicians were too. Punk still had a heartbeat at the end of the 1970s, and the punk attitude reigned supreme during a lot of those interviews. It was the first time TV had met rock on its own turf, and usually it was the band that was in control of the interview. They knew it, and it made them pretty cocky. They also knew enough about TV to push the limits. Consciously adding at least one "fuck" per sentence and punctuating it with a primordial spit could only help their image. In their world, that kind of behaviour was the norm, but to do it on TV was rebellion to the max. It may have been stupid and adolescent, but it was compelling to watch. This was real. It went to where rock and roll was really happening, where it really worked, and for an audience that was still under-age and unable to get into these clubs, the thrill of being there without leaving your rec room was undeniable. "The NewMusic" was far more instructive than Sunday dance shows for studying the language, the style, the code of cool kids are always so eager to understand.

What "The NewMusic" gained from putting itself through all these embarrassing hoops was hipness. (My guess is that was the last thing the musicians wanted to see happen to TV. They were hoping it would come off looking hopeless and square against their ultra-coolness.) Simply by sharing the same space as rock and roll, "The NewMusic" took on its personality. Its journalists became famous because of their proximity to the stars. The audience—still in the throes of old-think about TV's status—incorrectly assumed that simply being in the same room with Mick Jagger meant you were buddies, soulmates. And because the journalists straddled the rock world and the world in your rec room, they became accessible stars.

## moving songs

"The NewMusic" was a promising start in getting rock and roll on TV on its own terms. But getting TV to understand and advance the values of rock and roll (while not rejecting its own inherent bias towards commercialism) was, unfortunately, a pipe dream.

In the early 1980s, major labels decided that videos of their artists could accompany the release of albums and singles. It was a desperate attempt to buttress the fading rock market. Rock had ODed on pomposity—too many flash-pots, too much ego. Disco had taken over, and although we didn't know it, we were all waiting for the cleansing fires of punk to get rock back on track.

The music industry understood TV well enough to know that it was always thirsty for cheap new images of interest. In Canada, "The NewMusic" was just about the only venue for these videos, and while these four-minute, pre-edited advertisements made for much more easily produced shows, they were also drastically changing the whole point of TV programming.

The United States responded to the new product with MTV. To media moguls everywhere, video looked exciting—here was new, nifty programming provided virtually free of cost. But it was not without risks. True, video shows were "narrowcasted" programming, zapping into the lucrative teenage-to-twenty-five market, the market with all the disposable income. But it was also the first time there had been a channel exclusively for one demographic, and this was the demographic that still went downtown for its entertainment. Would they watch? Still, advertisers saw MTV as a licence to print money, and they desperately wanted a chance to be seen alongside the latest Duran Duran or Blondie video.

But it was a Faustian deal for rock and roll. Independent labels could rarely find the extra $15,000 needed for a video, while the major labels were creating bands with nothing but video in mind. Duran Duran is a prime example (although the band vehemently denies it—MTV was operating in only a few markets at the time, not enough of an audience to make stars out of them). Even in those earliest days, the record companies had figured out how to manipulate the medium. Duran Duran's "Girls on Film" tried out the "Banned in Boston" technique on MTV—if you get your work banned in one of America's most conservative cities, the notoriety will make it a hit across the rest of the country. It worked. From that point on, we all paid special attention to whatever that band offered—visually that is (the music was secondary in their case). The fabulous yachts and exotic locations were far better selling factors than the music was. This was the standard that very few major videos strayed from. (Peter Gabriel's "Sledgehammer" video was one of the few to actually have music that matched its stunning visuals.) In rock and roll on TV, TV was the big winner. The music was fading fast.

If only rock and roll had held out a little longer. If only it hadn't listened to the corporate interests and the push to compromise for the sake of sales. If only Citytv had realized that "The NewMusic" provided the perfect vehicle for translating rock and roll to TV and pushed that show in the United States and Britain. But they didn't, and the truth is, rock and roll only made it seriously (and almost fatally) to TV once the corporate poohbahs had confirmed that there was serious coinage to be made in the process.

In the first year of MuchMusic's operation (our Canadian all-music channel), Canadian sales of records sky-rocketed by 54 percent. That's serious marketing. While that was having a major effect in the business end of the music industry, the cultural impact of videos was even more powerful.

What music video did was dissolve the line between TV content and TV commercials—were you being sold something, or were you being entertained? It changed the way people make TV, and the way we watch it. Because the major shift in focus between programming and ads has been obliterated, we now give the commercials and the shows equal attention. Less muting for ads, no more waiting for the ads to get a beer or make a call. Nope, now the beer spots are just as interesting as the programs.

What's truly amazing to me is that the advertising business didn't come up with this idea themselves. The ad business is often thought to have all the respectability of pond scum. Why didn't some smart, ashamed ad exec see this way to turn out something that had all the outward appeal of art yet still sold Lemon Pledge? Advertising, however, caught on quickly. The winter of 1991-92 provided a classic example. Nirvana had catapulted to the top of the charts with a single called "Smells Like Teen Spirit." As it moved into high rotation at MuchMusic, commercials for a deodorant called Teen Spirit suddenly appeared, sometimes running immediately after the video. But neither the band nor the ad agency for Teen Spirit had anything to do with each other. Turns out the band did write the song in reference to the product (I can see why, "Smells Like Teen Spirit" is the best name for a song that I've heard in a long time) but not specifically to sell the product. The marketing manager for Mennen, the maker of Teen Spirit, said the fact that the company advertised heavily on MuchMusic just when the song became a big hit is pure coincidence. Well, maybe so, but a soon-to-catch-on shrewd marketing move is coming just around the corner. Watch for companies with new products to launch for the teenage market picking their product names from the top-ten charts, and for more bands stealing nifty product names and putting them in song titles. If they organize it right they can have their commercials playing while the song is still out there doing most of the work for them, or vice versa. There's got to be a lot of "contra" dealing here. The lawyers will be happy, and they will owe it all to music video, which first erased the line between content and commercial.

While this is a triumph for advertising on TV, it

also leaves the rock video audience with the distinct feeling that the program it is watching is exclusively a marketing exercise. In a way, this is great news. One small step for man, one giant step towards TV literacy. We are developing a critical eye for TV, leaving behind the passive attitude that kept us silent and on the couch for forty years. While network executives and advertisers may find us watching TV more intently, they know we'll zap away at the first hint that a show is talking down to us, its audience. We're literate enough to know exactly who a show is trying to reach, what demographic they're going for—and we don't have to see the commercials to figure that out. In a lot of ways, viewers could be way ahead of the network executives, and we're all beginning to understand what kind of power that offers. When you sit down to view the offerings of a new TV season and see networks busting butts and budgets to figure out what the viewers want (and how wrong they can be), it's laughable. To think that rock videos, in blurring the line between content and commercial, had a hand in all this is wonderful, and fitting, too. For rock and roll has offered almost every aspect of pop culture a new lease on life. And so it should—it's social, populist, sometimes thinking, sometimes juvenile, and able to change its mind at the drop of a beat.

## life expectancy

As time marches on, we rightly expect more and more out of TV. The changes to programming in rock on TV demonstrate this. The back-to-back video programming style of five years ago just doesn't hold viewers any more. It's no longer a great thrill to see our favourite artists on TV—they are there all the time, if not in their latest video, then on the newest Pepsi commercial or as guests on late night talk shows or on the news. Viewers demand more than that: they want to see where stars live, what their families look like, what they do in their spare time—we all want an all-access pass. And we've been getting it. "Entertainment Tonight," "Lifestyles of the Rich and Famous," the prime time specials of Oprah Winfrey and Barbara Walters all help to keep bums in seats. No longer content just to see the new video, we are now getting the full live concert. In some cases, we can see the tour on TV before it comes to our town. Optimistically, management wants to think that if we like it on TV we'll run out and buy a ticket. Realistically, it means that we don't have to buy a ticket and wait for the show to come to us—it already has.

If TV wants to hold a new, more TV-literate rock audience, its only hope is in creating rock events that can only happen on TV. Happenings that are equal parts "What is rock?" and "What is TV?" I have seen a hint of that.

Since the fall of 1991, MuchMusic has aired specials called "Intimate and Interactive." The premise is that a band comes into the studio with all their gear. For two hours they go live with a relaxed mix of performance and talk. Questions are provided by the studio audience, or the audience sitting in any of half a dozen pubs across the country that are linked up by satellite or by fax machine in the studio. This is kept moving by a VJ acting like a traffic cop. It's ground-breaking in two aspects. First, and most important to me, since it involves part of my livelihood, it virtually makes the job of host redundant. This show gives the audience direct access to the artist. No more processing through the presenter. That's the intimate part.

Second, the interactive part is done without the whiz technology we thought had to be in place to make TV interactive. "Intimate and Interactive" makes you part of the show—your questions, from your home town, your favourite hang-out, your phone. That's truly interactive.

TV presenters should be worried. Once you give that kind of control to an audience, they shouldn't want to give it back. This is a leap in demystifying TV. No longer will rock journalists enjoy fame by association, because now the kid down the block can talk with Mick Jagger too. The realization that anyone can be on TV has truly hit.

However, it takes a certain kind of artist to withstand the rigours of "Intimate and Interactive." So far, Mendelson Joe, Bruce Cockburn, Blue Rodeo, Daniel Lanois, Iggy Pop and the Barenaked Ladies have all stood up quite well, but many others would balk at the live aspect, and at the thought of being face to face with real people with real questions. They prefer the rock journalist jargon of TV types who are experts at playing the rock talk game but at the same time respect the musicians' privacy and reveal little about the person behind the music. Fans aren't like that; they're too random, too risky, too much like, well, like rock and roll.

Other than that example, there is little to show that TV understands it has fallen far behind its increasingly sophisticated audience. I'm tired of having to give what little credit exists for intelligent rock programming to Citytv and MuchMusic—would someone else get their act together please? Or perhaps the bloom is off the rose, demographics have shifted, record companies are wearying of supplying free programming to video networks, and maybe the viewers are wearying too—so no competitors are likely to emerge? For the most part, TV execs have failed to understand that rock and roll demands total involvement. For one thing, it's too loud to talk over. And yet, more often than not, rock on TV lies like a rug, on in the background, with people chatting guiltlessly over it. You watch TV sitting down; you go out to a rock concert, you're there with others, it's an event, you stand up for it. I'm always sorry to hear people talking the next day about last night's concert on MuchMusic. I can't help thinking, wouldn't it have been more fun if these people, all sitting staring at the same blue-tinted images in the privacy of their own homes, could have at least all got together and experienced it in each other's company? The same thing bothers me about Sony Walkmans—listening to rock music on a Walkman is essentially a contradiction in terms, and at heart antisocial and anti-rock. At least with a film you get some sense of being part of a social event.

And so, perhaps not too surprisingly, the glimmer of hope for rock and the moving pictures game comes from the big screen—in fact, the biggest screen.

When IMAX released *At the MAX with the Rolling Stones*, I celebrated. This film was truly better than being at the concert. Let's face it, no one paying retail can get tickets good enough to truly hear and see a mega rock show any more. As someone who's been lucky enough to have had the option, the place to see a great rock show is from the side of the stage. That's where you catch the egos, the energy, the mistakes and the laughs.

The sound at the IMAX film was better than anything TV could ever offer; and better than the rebounding slapback in some football stadium. Whatever instrument was on the screen was bumped up in the mix, just like in real life—if the camera was next to the saxophone, it's louder than anything else. There is something to be said for watching Jagger and Richards seventy-five-feet tall, but IMAX was smart enough to realize that the crowd element was just as crucial to the success of the film. The way the cameras were positioned in the audience gave you that slightly claustrophobic, sweaty feeling we've all come to expect. Add to that the real audience in the theatre who were there because they were Stones fans and digging the music, and the social element so important to rock's impact was nearly satisfied.

My biggest problem in watching *At the MAX* was that I wanted to get up and dance. I wanted to physically act out the concert atmosphere. So there is still room for improvement. Rock IMAX of the future should have a limited run, making it a special event like a rock concert. It should be in a huge warehouse, or outside in the summer on a slightly sloped floor. It should hold about eight hundred people, have chairs only at the back, and it should serve beer. Let the dancing begin! Let the live audience clap to pick the encores. They won't be able to complain about the seats and they'll get to dance and be surrounded by their friends.

This is where rock should be going. I think it's about ready to give up on TV. TV wants too much. TV wants rock and roll to be smart, pretty, funny, spontaneous and good TV—good music is incidental. IMAX, on the other hand, lets musicians do what they do best—play.

Whither rock and roll on TV? I suppose the futurists and cyberpunks would agree that the trend that sees technology becoming increasingly interactive will mean the ability to build your own superband for a superconcert: you pick the musicians, living or dead; you pick the program, the venue; and you can probably even stage the inevitable end-of-concert, everyone-on-stage version of "I Shall Be Released," and it won't sound any worse than it usually does, either.

Will these superconcerts of the future have anything to do with rock and roll? Probably no more than TV ever has. The two are really antithetical. Cain and Abel all over again. They've done interesting battle from time to time and "The NewMusic" fought one of the more equal matches. There may be more "adult-oriented" music video stations in future, appealing to the aging boomers, but this won't really have anything to do with rock and roll either. With more impressive stereos and quads being hooked onto "home theatre" screens, you might hope that watching rock on TV will make a go of it, but there is an inherent contradiction involved. Despite its ever-growing screen size, TV is shrinking—becoming more personal, more like a work-tool, telling you about your bank balance and airline schedule, showing you the videos of your kids. Narrowcasting is the future, and it's essentially less communal, with less money for programming, meaning smaller shows. Rock and roll may be showing its age, but it isn't shrinking. It is still what it has always been, larger than life, variously a chimera, a joke, a call to arms, a call to tears, a vote for life, sexual and powerful. It is far more than technology. It is far more than business. It is far more than TV.

# rock of ages

in which we learn what rock does best and who still remembers what that is

At its heart, rock and roll is about teenagers, and then, mostly about teenage sex. It is also about rebellion, but then, of course, so is teenage sex. It is, by definition, music that parents do not like. When parents like it, it stops being rock and roll and becomes "golden oldies" or "easy listening" or some other programming cliché. It is constantly new, eternally young, and must be reinvented several times a decade. It has also been an alternate NHL in the dreams of several generations of Canadian kids. It offers the hope of vast riches to lower-class kids. It even offers a hint of political awareness to those who can hear the lyrics above the din.

According to Pete Townshend, rock and roll and "the teenage condition" are one and the same. As he told MuchMusic's Christopher Ward, rock and roll is about being "angry, violent, miserable, whining, complaining, unhappy, frustrated, desperate, and being happy about it."

Pete came up with that one about five years ago. He, unlike a lot of other middle-aged rock stars, has not forgotten what it was like to be a teenager. It's about contradicting yourself, swinging wildly between absolute self-confidence and debilitating self-doubt. But these days you have to look hard to find music in the top ten that reflects that kind of agonizing teenage experience. The teenage condition has been battered underground.

Teenagers have always been an underdog generation but never as much as now. Today, they are vastly outnumbered by the aging baby-boomer generation—the generation that feels it owns rock and roll, the generation that has forced rock to age along with it. Everything has been skewed to the older rock market. Even the technology we listen to music on, the CD, is too often out of the price range of most teenagers. It's their parents who buy the CDs; teens are the cassette market. In refusing to give up the music of their youth to the next generation, the baby-boomers have effectively pushed teenagers out of the music charts that were originally targetted to them alone.

From the moment punk was finished, all the anger and discontent that goes along with the teenage experience disappeared from the airwaves. Musicians got responsible. They wanted to feed children, save the rain forest, save farms. There was no room for the self-centred, destructive music of teenagers. What purpose did it serve? If it wasn't contributing to some larger good, it was dismissed as unimportant. But, in fact, that very same self-obsessed, whining teenage rock serves a very important purpose. Not only for the kids who are able to say "Finally, here's something that's mine," but as a barometer of their mood.

In the search for something that teenagers can call their own today, something that parents hate, rap and house music (music made primarily for dancing to), hardcore and thrash and grunge were born. But for all the success rap has enjoyed (the biggest breakthrough being that a truly black form of music, performed by blacks, finally hit top-ten pop radio), it still felt like a transitional phase. Historically, dance music has filled the gap while rock caught its breath and reinvented itself. (Remember the state rock music was in when disco hit? Barry Manilow was in the top ten, for God's sake!) Rap is a cultural pillager—interesting, ironically unique, but not a contender to replace rock and roll. It relies too much on existing musical form (mostly from music already recorded). And now, the baby-boomers are now appropriating rap and house for their own. It's been dubbed the "rebirth of cool," and with the rap slowed down and the addition of live instruments playing ripped-off licks from the hits of the jazz world, rap in this new form is being enjoyed by the hip and forty crowd over fancy dinners. It's the sound of the beat generation they were born too late to enjoy. So much for teenage innercity angst.

As a form of popular music, rock and roll has lasted longer than most. So now that dance music hits the charts once again, popular culture vultures are asking the question: is rock finally dead? The big irony is that when it does die, few will notice or care. Because for it to expel its last, tired, beer-stinking breath, it must be replaced by a new music, one that is young and has found the passion that rock and roll has been recycling for the last fifteen years.

Rock is not dead, but it is certainly a different beast than when I first started listening. Rock has lost its balance. It has toppled too far to the right of centre by getting into bed with corporate interests (both recording and advertising). That has alienated a lot of old fans, but it has also brought a whole new mainstream demographic into the tent. Rock has lost most of the integrity it was rumoured to have had, and transmogrified into a crazed capitalist carnivore that can take a bite out of every medium around. From grandmothers flocking to buy Rick Astley's Christmas album to four-year-olds at New Kids on the Block concerts, rock and roll has something to sell everybody.

## rock's moral majority

In the mid-1980s a new campaign was launched to try to cover rock's transparent greedy motives. Rock, we are told, grew a conscience. Now, rock has certainly always been self-conscious, but rock with a conscience? What the hell does that mean? Looking it up in the *Oxford Dictionary*, the old-style rock and roll certainly falls under meanings 1 and 2:

1. Inward knowledge of consciousness; internal conviction;

2. Inmost thought; mind, heart.

But meaning number 3 is what "conscience" in rock is all about;

3. The internal recognition of the moral quality of one's motives and actions; the faculty or principle which pronounces upon the moral quality of one's actions or motives, approving the right and condemning the wrong.

*Approving the right and condemning the wrong.* Morals, rights and wrongs—this is where the balance has been lost in rock and roll. Although rock through its brief history has always been a place for lamenting big wrongs—Bob Dylan, Michelle Shocked and the Clash built their careers on it—good rock has also sometimes been able to maintain an artistic view that gave the negative and the positive equal time, with no moral condemnation attached to either. A song about the despair of heroin addiction by Lou Reed, or sexual obsession with a blow-up doll by Roxy Music, could and did evoke the same response as a love ballad. Rock has always been open-minded enough to find beauty in grotty situations. Death is as appealing as life. Rock was a good forum for this kind of artistic balance, for it was innately understood that you didn't bring your morals to this stuff. You brought your eyes, your ears and your heart, and you were paid off with an experience and an understanding of experiences you yourself were unlikely to have. (I've never been into heroin or blow-up dolls, but those songs have left me unwilling to make a moral judgment on those who are.)

I can even remember the day I heard the door shut on rock's seesaw ride between heaven and hell. It was 1986, and XTC were in the MuchMusic studio to promote their new album and single "Dear God." I had done an interview with Andy Partridge for "The NewMusic" and it had gone very well. (Never pass up a chance to interview a smart musician, they come around all too infrequently.) I then handed him over to Much for a live interview on air with Erica Ehm. Erica easily got Andy to admit that he did not believe in God. Her eyes got very wide, the whole studio got uncomfortably quiet, and the decision to roll another video came down, signifying to me that speaking with a musician on music TV who did not believe in God was too over-the-top, too radical. It was at that moment I realized that the audience out there probably thought this was unacceptable stuff too. I went to the washroom and wept. I bet Andy Partridge was silently weeping as well, as he suffered through the rest of the interview on the ever-so-hip but ever-so-conservative cowhide-upholstered couch. That was the one couch in the nation from which Andy should have been able to speak about his music without fear, and I know we disappointed him. Much and its audience pretend they are an underground, slightly rebellious group that lives a rock and roll life; nothing could be further from the truth. In the age of moral-majority boycott groups, the cheekiness of "Dear God" was beyond the pale. For me, that was the day that irony, metaphor and dreaming had a price placed on its head.

While some bands were suffocating under this newfound conscience, others had grown wings and were hitting new natural highs with well-intentioned top-ten songs. Simple Minds were one of the first serious, positive, conscience-driven bands to arrive on earth, one of the "if you can't say something nice, don't say nothing at all" bands. I got to talk to Jim Kerr at a hometown gig in Glasgow in 1987.

It was an amazing concert. First of all it was played in Ibrox stadium, a football venue and a tribal sepulchre of Protestant obsession. This Simple Minds concert marked the first time a Catholic from Glasgow had appeared on that stage. It was a very big deal, to both the audience and Jim Kerr. As a Canadian, it's hard for me to fully understand how important that was, but the atmosphere pre-show let me know. There was more singing going on in the stands than there was on stage—not Simple Minds songs, football anthems. That's not unusual at European shows, but at this show everybody was singing the anthems for both the Catholic and the Protestant teams. When Jim Kerr arrived on stage he joined in and led everyone in another round of cheers. He played the "rock with a conscience" role to saintly proportions. After all, as his hit single declared, "he promised us a miracle," and a Catholic playing Ibrox was certainly a miracle to the Glaswegians.

Backstage, Kerr had conflicting emotions about the whole deal. The euphoria of the hometown crowd had certainly left him on a high, but he was celebrating that high all alone in the Protestant showers that served as his dressing room. I asked him why his music was so one-sided, so unbalanced, seemingly so sugar-coated. He agreed it was heavily weighted on the positive side but he explained that he wrote that way consciously hoping to use his music to balance the dark side of real life in Glasgow—the unemployment, the poverty, the drug problems, the general hopelessness. He thought he was offering a service, and now that he had started, he felt he couldn't stop. (They won't let him stop. Jim Kerr's name is still at the top of the phone list for concerts with a cause.)

It sounds like a very nice thing to do, sticking to the sunny side of the street, but it disturbed the balance rock music was built on. Bands like Simple Minds created a fantasy world instead of finding beauty in reality—something you'd expect more from the flaky end of folk, not rock and roll. Simple Minds started out making music for teenagers, but lost them when the music began to be about something other than the world they lived in.

The true beginning of rock with conscience had to be Live Aid. I'd be an idiot to say that the first worldwide charity concert was a bad idea, but no one, not even Saint Bob Geldoff, could have foreseen what a negative impact charity gigs would have on rock in the near future.

I was riveted to the TV for the entire concert. Except for the embarrassing pleas for money from Sally Field (if I heard her say "one more drop in the bucket" one more time, I was going to need a bucket myself), the Live Aid event was a powerful marriage of the rock and the wired world. For much of its existence, rock and roll has been denied, sat on by the status quo, told it has no real power or relevancy or true importance because it is about adolescent concerns. But Live Aid showed both the powers that be and the musicians themselves that their power and influence was undeniable, and, on a global level, unrivalled. It blasted off the TV. The looks on the faces of the musicians tell it all. Ask anyone today who performed at Live Aid and they'll get goosebumps just thinking about it.

It changed the look and intent of rock forever. For many non-rock fans, it also gave rock a credibility it never had before. While a good part of Live Aid's TV audience would never have gone to the live concert in either London or Philadelphia, they could watch these bands at home and, for the first time, understand what they were trying to do. It no longer had to do with teenage antics and a fascination with glamour. These musicians had a global agenda and global concerns that could be understood by everyone, not just a teenage rock fan.

The technology employed by Live Aid is what has really changed rock and roll. The ability to be instantaneous and world-wide is painting a very different picture for rock in the future. World tours are exhausting and increasingly less profitable. With the technology available, why not negotiate a world-wide deal with a production company, mount one fantabulous live show, shoot it to death, transmit it live and make it a global event? No more disappointing sound in hockey arenas, no competing for ticket money with other touring acts, no wear and tear on the voice and the body, and much less of a security risk as well. This may not be the case for Europe, where major cities are so close together and touring is much more profitable, but for the United States and especially for Canada (where many artists play only two or three dates because of the incredible distances between urban centres), it makes a lot of sense.

The other ground-breaking consciousness-raiser was Artists United Against Apartheid's 1985 release, *Sun City*. A record that was destined to fail on pop radio in the U.S. (it sounded too black and was far too political, especially for the Southern states, where it was never heard on radio) became an instant expression of the antiracism zeitgeist and did more than any U.N. deterrent to shrink the blacklist of performers who continued to perform in South Africa. It was a hit, despite the fact that none of the artists involved had ever been asked to play Sun City and that 97 percent of the artists continued to receive royalties from their South African record sales.

After Live Aid and *Sun City*, the enthusiasm and support for charity gigs got completely unplugged. Let's face it, things got way out of hand. Farm Aid, Sport Aid, Prince's Trust, Self Aid, Jamaica Aid, Ferry Aid—I started to feel really abused watching and working at these things. Not only was I expected to shell out money for each cause of the moment, but every performer was hoping I was going to shell out for their latest album, too. Think about it—one single live performance to forty thousand people, and maybe another million or so by satellite—that saves a lot of road rubber in promoting an album. As soon as record companies and managers figured out that enticing bit of financial information, they weren't waiting for calls to be asked to participate in a charity concert. They were calling and offering services.

In England more than anywhere else, things quickly turned ugly. Loads of one-hit-wonder pop stars were accused of propping up their pointless careers by keeping their faces in the public eye through charity videos. It's easier to drop down to a studio once a month, sing one line of a song someone else wrote and look pretty for the video than it is to write a new album and spend three months in the studio trying to pull it off. It was a brand-new way to have pop star status without ever really producing anything.

The focus of the charities changed. Instead of benefitting the cause of starving, helpless children, the concert for Ferry Aid raised money in the name of partygoers drowned in the Thames. As Midge Ure (musical director for the Prince's Trust concerts) put it, "There was a charity gig for anyone who fell down and scraped their knee." He refused to have any part. The charity backlash started in the musical community. When Aussie soap star Kylie Minogue performs at a John Lennon benefit concert in Liverpool, you know it's all over. Many rock stars were getting reputations as do-gooders, taking the moralistic high road. For many of them, that didn't jibe very well with the rock lifestyle they were pushing when not doing charity gigs. They were looking like frauds. Many faded out of the charity circuit and went back to work. They realized that the pop charity industry was about money and influence, not about music and fans.

The goodwill and camaraderie that was evident at Live Aid didn't last too long, either. At the Nelson Mandela birthday charity concert, there were more political moves being made backstage than there were on stage. This was the concert where the artists lost control of the event. Originally promoted as a "Free Mandela" event, it quickly became no more than a birthday party after TV networks threatened to pull the plug on any political content. The artists went along with it and by doing so lost the power that Live Aid had shown the world rock could have. Meanwhile, backstage, terrible rumours surfaced about Whitney Houston refusing to let Stevie Wonder use her equipment when his failed to show up, and then when he finally did get on, Houston supposedly made him cut his act short because he was cutting into her time. That's the spirit! (Actually, the one good thing about the Mandela concert is that, for the first time, there were almost enough black acts on the bill. Not quite enough to avoid press saying there weren't, but the Mandela gig was a better mix than most of the charity happenings.)

Big names would not do a gig unless other big names were also confirmed. I guess the logic was that if they were the only supergroup in the line-up, they would look like they were backing a loser charity gig. Stars would not do duets with anyone lower on the totem pole than they were. Where they performed in the line-up, rebroadcast rights, home video rights, merchandizing rights—all these things had to be negotiated beforehand. This was hard business, not goodwill.

And where were the young, new voices of rock and roll metal? This truly teen music was rarely included in any charity venture, mostly because of the musical snobbery of the pop musicians in charge of the events, but also because their inclusion didn't make a lot of sense to the programmers. Heavy metal was the one type of music that continued to refuse to make moralistic judgments, that continued to be adolescent. Metal was dealing more and more in the murky, dark side of life, sex and death. Somehow combining an Anthrax gig with a charity to put eyeglasses on children in Africa didn't work. But after a year or two of being excluded, the spandex-and-hairspray crowd got a little grumpy, especially when they realized the numbers of people these events were seen by. In 1986 they retaliated with a charity record of their own. *Here'n Aid* is definitely a collectors' item with widdely-widdely guitar players trying to outdo each other and singers popping blood vessels to get the best scream on the record. Metal charity failed to get off the ground. Besides the risk of aneurysm, bands quickly realized it would do little for their image. Their job—to be the bad boys of rock—was more important now than ever, because pop musicians were sounding and acting more and more like Ozzie and Harriet all the time.

## "smells like teen spirit"

Perhaps it was inevitable that along with a paunch rock would grow a conscience. All the big rock stars were getting old. All the biggies were over forty with wives, kids, big houses, big responsibilities and plenty of employees. The "live fast, die young and leave a beautiful corpse" attitude was replaced in their mid-thirties with "I must leave a better world for my children, quit smoking and get my eyes lifted." They couldn't act like teenagers any more, or their teens might, too. As parents, they had to set an example, and that attitude drifted over to the music pretty quickly. That's okay for the rock audience that are also parents, but is a teenager going to put up with that? A lot did. In plenty of Canadian households, there was no generation gap when it came to what got put on the CD player. Mom's Michael Jackson discs ended up in Sarah's bedroom often enough.

On the other hand, for those teens who didn't relate to Phil Collins or Mariah Carey, the underground options got delightfully grimy. I came face to face with the grimiest of the lot from 1987 to 1990 when I hosted MuchMusic's "PowerHour," the weekly hard rock video show. MuchMusic had always had trouble finding someone who wanted to host the show, so they were surprised but glad when I said I wanted to do it. Heavy metal was one of the last arenas where one could find real teenage music. I much preferred its angry, extremely loyal and particularly crazy fans to dealing with the fans of the latest scrubbed teen sensation who would write New Kids on the Block one thousand times on a piece of paper and send it to RSVP on MuchMusic in hopes we would play their video.

Heavy metal has never had the integrity of punk (whose motto was think and act for yourself). In a way, it's the lazy rebel's music. A form of escape more than anything else, it doesn't want kids to do anything, it simply offers a way out of their problems. It's all horror, hormones, smoke-bombs and guillotines, and the assurance that if you truly like all this stuff, you indeed are one of the aliens you always suspected you were.

The mail from the "PowerHour" was fascinating. In many instances, I knew I was holding the first letter that teen had ever written. While the Rick Astley fan was only concerned that each Rick Astley she wrote looked identical to the last, the molten-metal kid from North Battleford, Saskatchewan, spent a week on his letter making sure it was as full of personality and wit as he could muster. A lot of the mailbag for the "PowerHour" came from prisons across the country. It took me a while to decipher the jail-speak, but the slang was virtually the same nation-wide, and the tone of the letters was always serious, and in their own way quite respectful and sweet. I loved these letters.

To: Miss Laurie Jane Brown
September 11, 1987

> Hi my name is Ken Mason. I watched power—yesterday thursday sep 10/87. And it was great. You should have more Kiss AC DC White Snake. My requst for the next power our is by The Outfield—play deep—and the song is for you Laurie Brown. I think you the best one on Much Music. And you have very beautiful eyes. I wish I could meet you. But I'm in jail right now, till Feb 88. I'm in

Drumheller Pen in Alberta Cannada. I want you to play something For the Boys Down here in Drumheller Pen, you pick the song Laurie, Make sure its real hard rock song.

I hope you can understand this letter, I don't write to good because I have a learning problem, Its called deslexcia, I can't read or write to good. So sorry if you can't read it. Oh ya, are you married and if not would you like to be. /yes or no/ Or how would like to be my pen pal if you do write please send me a picture TV. I'll tell you a bit about myself, I'm 24, 5'11", blonde hair, blue eyes and well built, I'm right into lifting weights. I get out soon and I'll be coming down there to visit a few friends of mine. Oh ya, I ride a bike 1985 soft tail Harley Davidson. Well Laurie, I got to go so take care, write soon please, see you in the near future maybe, I hope so.

Yours truly,
Ken Mason

In metal, the fans are the same as the musicians—there is very little separating the kids on stage from the kids in the club. They could switch places easily. This translates into some very heavy bonding between band and fan. The possibility that the guy in the audience could find himself on stage within a year with a band like he's watching right now is not out of the question. They would not do it only for the money, but for the fun, and to look cool in front of their friends.

Interviewing metal maniacs gave me an idea of what it must have been like trying to do TV interviews in the punk heyday. Not willing to play the TV game, like punkers, heavy-metal guys were generally unresponsive, somewhat obnoxious, and always unreliable. (What a breath of fresh air after your top ten artist, who would do anything you asked in the name of TV exposure.) They also didn't have much opportunity to get on television. Their videos consistently inspired mail from upset parents when we tried to include them in the regular programming, so hardcore and metal was ghettoized to half an hour a day. Because it's underground music, no one but the "PowerHour" was interested in talking to them on TV. Bands like Megadeth and Metallica (the best of the bunch) didn't build their fan base from TV exposure, so, in turn, they didn't need it. There is a kind of integrity that surrounds these bands because of that. These guys had been on the road for years, playing the worst clubs, sleeping in the dirtiest vans, making the least money and having the best time any teenager could dream of. It's obvious their music was more important to them than anything else. It stood for something. They revelled in the fact that not only did Phil Collins fans hate it, their own parents hated it. Heavy metal was a huge, ugly monster separating kids from parents: the more they thought about it, if their parents hated the music that they so definitely identified with, by extension, their parents must hate them (and vice versa).

Any good teenage band is full of the contradictions that make up the wacky world of youth. In the front of the Megadeth tour bus, Dave Mustaine told me how important his reading is to him and how upset he is about the number of illiterate kids in the United States. Meanwhile, in the back of the bus, the rest of the band was watching a truly digusting porn video and trying to have a democratic debate about the band's only road rule "don't come in the box." (They worried more about paternity suits than world population, I would guess.) People no longer connected to the teenage world would look at this situation and dismiss these guys entirely—the back of the bus cancels out anything positive that's going on up front. But that is the infinitely interesting way the teenage mind works; in spite of the contradictions, both types of behaviour coexist semi-peacefully. Just don't ask them to rationalize it.

In meeting these bands, I got the sense they felt like Billy Graham on crusade, bringing their message to kids looking for something to relate to, kids who were beginning to think they didn't belong on this planet, that the society they lived in didn't have any room for the way they thought and felt. These bands would blow into town and in effect say, "I know exactly how you feel, I feel that way too. You're not crazy. You're damn right to be angry, and you should feel proud of your anger."

The swagger, the half-lidded "I'm too hungover to notice anything" look of these bands (and their fans) makes parents and music programmers alike think these people are generally stem-dead. But mostly these bands are passionate about life. Everything, from washing their hair to driving to the next gig, is done with limitless passion and energy, and that's what separates them from most pop bands.

Amazingly enough, there are a few dinosaur bands that still understand the teenage passion. Rob Halford, from Judas Priest, is one of the best at this; he's also one of the most intelligent. (Judas Priest is the band whose music seems to be most often blamed for suggesting suicide to its listeners.) The complete antithesis of a heavy-metal lead singer, Rob (over forty and rumoured to be gay) feels an unbelievable loyalty and concern for his fans. Their frustration and anger is mounting, he says. When he comes out on stage, the tension in the air is frightening. It's a powder-keg situation, and he feels that it's his job to diffuse it. Blackie Lawless, from the now defunct Wasp, said the same thing. He said his job was as much psychologist as singer. He felt he was doing parents a favour by tapping into the wounded, dark corners of the teenage brain, bringing out the pain and anger and dealing with it. This release of teenage frustration has always been at the heart of rock and roll. It's my guess that Pete Townshend demolishing his guitar on stage stopped a lot of kids from taking their frustrations out on other people's cars on the way home.

Up until the mid-1980s, metal was considered, by most fans and non-fans of the music, to be fun, stupid, exhilarating and passionate. Then, in the space of about a year, metal became dangerous and damaging music. The metal bands looked on the social responsibility of bands like Simple Minds and U2, rock's new conscience-ridden preachers, as so unnatural and so out of tune with the real world that they responded with a gag and a knee-jerk reaction. In the face of all the top-of-the-charts optimism, heavy metal saw the teenage world falling apart. AIDS was changing everything. Sex, the best and cheapest way to have fun, was being taken away from them. So were jobs. Nothing these almost-spiritual bands sang about made any real sense. U2 sang "Once More In the Name of Love." Sure, thought the metal fan, but with a condom on. At the same time your radio was blasting "You Promised Us a Miracle," Oral Roberts was saying the exact same thing as he blackmailed his flock of sheep with threats from his accountant, God. It all looked hopeless and hypocritical to the hard rock fan.

Metal retaliated by trying to counterbalance the views the rest of the rock world had taken. The music did get more violent and depressing beyond belief, but in the eyes of the teenage metal fan, that reflected his own feelings about his world and his non-future. In 1985, these metal bands quickly found themselves the subject of U.S. Senate hearings spearheaded by the Washington, D.C.-based Parents Music Resource Center (PMRC), spearheaded by now Second Lady Tipper Gore.

She contended that rock music "has taken a radical turn...much of it is blatantly obscene and violent and projects activities, values and behaviour corrosive to young minds and a healthy population." She cited examples from Judas Priest, Mötley Crüe, Prince, Sheena Easton, Wasp, and The Captain and Tennille ("Do That to Me One More Time") and Springsteen ("I'm on Fire"). Oh brother! While Prince and Springsteen did not attend the hearings, passionate statements against the PMRC were given by Frank Zappa, John Denver and Dee Snider of Twisted Sister.

What the PMRC wanted out of the hearings was a rating system that would warn parents of "offensive" material. Many of the band members whose material was made an example of at the senate hearings will tell you that their subsequent recordings were deliberately even more "offensive" simply to infuriate the PMRC. Lyrics became lists of the dirtiest words that anyone could think of, strung back to back. Tell a teenager he can't do something, and he'll do it.

The late Frank Zappa (although never on the PMRC list for offensive material) responded with a ratings sticker of his own. It read:

> This album contains material which a truly free society would neither fear nor suppress. In some socially retarded areas, religious fanatics and ultra-conservative political organizations violate your First Amendment Rights by attempting to censor rock and roll albums. We feel that this is un-Constitutional and un-American. As an alternative to these government-supported programs (designed to keep you docile and ignorant), Barking Pumpkin is pleased to provide stimulating digital audio entertainment for those of you who have outgrown the ordinary. The language and concepts contained herein are guaranteed not to cause eternal torment in the place where the guy with the horns and the pointed stick conducts his business. This guarantee is as real as the threats of the video

fundamentalists who use attacks on rock music in their attempt to transform America into a nation of check-mailing nincompoops (in the name of Jesus Christ). If there is a hell, its fires waits for them, not us.

Dear, wonderful Frank!

If only Tipper Gore had read a few history books before she launched her senators' wives coffee-klatch, she would have realized that at any time in the past when the forces of censorship have raised their ugly heads, it only served to increase the amount of "offensive" material it was trying to stop. What Tipper didn't understand is that even teens have a critical sense (when left on their own to develop it), and if they hadn't been pressured, they would probably have come to the realization, all by themselves, that some of these bands had gone too far.

The scary thing about the PMRC was how much influence they had. In November 1985, the Recording Industry Association of America (a music industry organization representing more than twenty record labels) agreed to a warning-sticker campaign. It wasn't far enough for Tipper, but it tried to balance the artists' freedom of expression with the senators' wives calling for castration.

In the end, enthusiasm and support dwindled for the PMRC. Their argument ventured too far into right-wing fundamentalist behaviour for the music industry and music fans to handle. Tipper has greatly changed her tune since the PMRC hearings. Where was she for the great "Cop Killer" incident in 1992? (Ice-T's provocative song from his *Body Count* album launched police demonstrations and calls for boycotts against Warner, his record company, and court action against retailers for selling the record.) Tipper was busy on the campaign for her vice-presidential husband, during which she declared that she really loved rock and roll and had even played drums in a band once.

At MuchMusic it was an extremely difficult time. Any good rock-and-roller loathes the idea of censorship, but how to keep the "PowerHour" on the air without succumbing to the all-too-easy way out of simply refusing to play the controversial music? I have always leaned towards the "let art go where it must—it is in the eye and ear of the beholder to sort things out" attitude (known in the other camp as opting out). I never wanted anything censored. Of the truly offensive videos (I'd say about 30 percent of them), half looked like bad horror films with lots of blood, while the other half were crammed with the worst examples of both violence against women and female stereotyping that you could imagine. The rest of them were just dorky. Bad metaphors for penises using guns, stick shifts and motorcycles.

We ended up giving our audience the choice. We'd play the video once and ask them to write and tell us what they thought. It always worked—their letters proved to me that they were definitely critical of what they were looking at and pleased to be given the chance to have some input into the programming. I also encouraged them to write to the bands of the offending videos and tell them what they thought. It's a standard business premise: one letter represents many customers. If the band got written feedback from fans (or potential fans) that their video was offensive, you could be sure the record company would think twice next time.

By 1988 this kind of cautionary introduction was necessary for about 50 percent of what we were playing. It was getting ridiculous, and I was tired of asking the audience did they perceive any "stereotyping," "degrading behaviour" or "pointless violence" in the videos. While MuchMusic was trying hard not to offend its audience, heavy metal bands were making videos aimed at turning parents and non-metal fans ballistic. It was a no-win situation. This is where hardcore and thrash stepped in to save the day. While videos for this music had been around since 1985, in 1989 they took over from the hair-sprayed, leopard-skin crowd. Metal had self-destructed in its effort to counteract the right-wing mainstream, and the door was wide open for something new. Thrash was louder, faster, more cynical and much more aggressive—it could suck the breath right out of you. If parents found the sound of metal music grating, this stuff was migraine material. But thrash and hardcore were thought of as the thinking man and woman's metal. Provided with a lyric sheet, I found that proved true.

What do you mean,"I don't believe in God"?
I talk to him everyday.
What do you mean, "I don't support your system"?
I go to court when I have to.

What do you mean, "I can't get to work on time"?
I got nothing better to do.
And, what do you mean, "I don't pay my bills"?
Why do you think I'm broke? Huh?
If there's a new way
I'll be the first in line.
But, it better work this time.

Megadeth
"Peace Sells...But Who's Buying?"

Hardcore realized early on in the game that the real world was much more morbid than anything a metal band could fantasize about, so they stuck to the facts. Lyrics were radically nihilistic, a look at everything that was wrong with the world.

Not only was the music now more aggressive—with the beat doubled it sounded more like machine-gun fire than rock and roll—the physicality of the performance was truly awesome. It was the complete abandon of the band and the audience that drove home the *raison d'être* for hardcore. Aggressive release. Articulate as it was, it had another grammar. Moshing, slam-dancing, head-butting, stage-diving—this was a way of saying how you felt without using words, words that people on the outside found dangerous. These audiences were all willing participants, and miraculously the injuries were few and far between. A lot of the pit antics in clubs seemed borrowed from punk, but punk was a British experience. The hardcore crowd was head-butting for different reasons. Hardcore was truly American, and not as far away from the stereotypical teenage experience as one might think. As Jello Biafra, the granddaddy of hardcore, explained it, "In high school football, they tell you to go out there and do it for the coach. I'm here to say there is no coach—do it for yourself."

While in Britain punk was the total denial of everything that was social reality (and by denying everything, it made anything possible) in North America no one wanted to go that far. The hardcore world-view was certainly as apocalyptic as punk's, but North America couldn't make the giant, liberating leap of refusal that the Brits had. Hardcore preferred to wallow in its social condition rather than obliterate it.

As with punk in the late 1970s, with hardcore and thrash in the late 1980s, rock was able to eke out another stay of execution. Curfew shall not ring tonight! The underground was alive again, living for the moment and adding a new chapter to the family album. Metal, meanwhile, softened up bigtime. It changed its name to "hard rock" and put out pompous rock anthems that had more to do with pop music than metal (witness Bon Jovi). Most of the really disgusting lyrics and videos were gone, replaced instead by overblown egos and hair (again, Bon Jovi). Hard rock videos looked more and more like beer commercials, and because of that, the music was easier to buy and sell. They even put out ballads, for God's sake.

Hard rock was mainstream; it sounded more than vaguely familiar, which meant any old rock-and-roller from the 1960s was ripe for reviving. I can't tell you how many times I had to remind the Much audience that Led Zeppelin was around before the video age and that was why we weren't "playing enough of them."

## jurassic rock

I have never been able to fully understand how the dinosaurs find their way back onto the pop charts. Why is it that most people have a musical alarm clock that goes off in their early thirties, and from that point onward all subsequent music fails to measure up to what's known? That alarm clock sounds the death knell for any further interest in new music (except if it sounds exactly like old music). Sure, everyone loves the soundtrack of their youth, it can kick-start a lot of potent memories, but why does musical adventurousness have to end? I have a secret feeling that for these people, the teenage years were the best years of their lives, and constantly listening to that music reminds them of younger and happier times. How unfortunate if your teenage years were your best; I remember feeling awkward, stupid and terribly confused. Since then I have added other emotions, concerns and frustrations to that list of feelings that I want my music to address. My only guess is that the people who have stopped listening to anything new have also stopped thinking about the music they do listen to. They don't want their music to be difficult any more—only there to supply an underscore to their lives.

Just around the time heavy metal music was dying in the late 1980s, the older baby-boomer generation found there was something lacking in the music their peers were making. Sure, they had enough radio stations—"Classic radio," "we only spin gold," "easy listening," "light radio" (to go along with their light beer) but the playlists were getting a little threadbare. The whole New Age sound that was expected to fill that gap never came down from the clouds long enough to make an impact. (Besides, you can't sing along to that stuff. I'm always very wary of any piano music that sounds like I could sit down and play it with my eyes shut.) VH1, the video network targeting an older demographic in the States, had it even tougher than radio. Sure, there was a lot of soft new stuff on the market, but not enough, and there weren't any videos made when The Eagles and Poco were in high gear, which is what their audience really wanted to see and hear.

All over California, there were overly tanned, slightly paunchy, retired rock stars with highlighted long shags, and they could hear the ring of distant cash registers. Nostalgia's here, and the time is right for picking the same pockets we picked fifteen years ago. Call up the other aged members; everyone lose twenty pounds; hire an image consultant and a video director and off we go again. This time, with the highly organized world of music television, the one thing that would have given them away as has-been musicians, the body-battering touring schedule, could be completely avoided. Most of these groups stipulated in their contracts that they would not tour extensively.

Yes, Procol Harem, Wings, and The Monkees for God's sake. The frustration of having to interview them just about killed me. The temptation to say, "So, who the hell asked you to get back together?" was always on the tip of my rapidly-turning-bitter tongue. The only thing these people wanted to talk about was the fact that there was no good music around any more, and out of respect for rock and roll they thought it was their duty to flog it one more time. In some ways they were right. If the generation that was supposed to be in control of popular music was blowing it, why shouldn't they step back in and show the kids how it's done? But none of them had the nerve to say, "I'm cashing in big on the nostalgia thing. I'm taking the money and running. You kids today don't deserve anything better, obviously, or you would have come up with it yourselves!"

I don't have a problem with the Monkees touring—they never expected us to believe that they had any credibility—but the Poco reunion of 1990 was the end for me. It's only the artists who never stopped writing and working that I have any time for. Robert Plant, who (so far) refuses a Led Zep reunion and continues to write valid songs with relevant lyrics for an audience that apparently isn't interested and wants him instead to wallow in nostalgia doing Zeppelin material, has my sympathy. Right now Plant is digging his heels in and refuses to recreate his past, but as each solo album sells fewer and fewer units, the financial possibilities of putting it back together can't be easy to walk away from.

I have the same kind of respect for the Stones. While their newer albums sound very much like any other Stones album, the fact that they continue to do solo albums of very different-sounding stuff tells me they are still musically alive and willing to take the risk of doing something their fans may not like. They've embraced new technology and new performers.

This wave of nostalgia certainly doesn't belong exclusively to one g-g-g-generation, or exclusively to the listeners. Once when my father was in town, I took him to see Gene DiNovi play the lounge at the King Edward Hotel. DiNovi recognized my father (who had at one point been Oscar Peterson's piano-tuner) and came and sat with us. I'm not sure he knew what I did but before long he was telling me that there had not been one note of worthy music written since Gershwin (presumably including his own compositions, which includes the theme song for "The Dick Van Dyke Show"). Not only had he stopped listening, he had pronounced music dead.

Perhaps the swing around to nostalgia can be taken as a good sign, a sign that things need to change. Until that change surfaces, people will continue to fall back on the familiar, the music that can make them feel young and powerful once again, the re-treaded calm before the storm.

## rock's rightful owners

After years of suffering the reign of the dinosaurs, it looks like the Ice Age may be approaching for these bands. Guns N' Roses were the first group to take a good kick at the fat cats in 1987. They put the bad boys back into rock and roll, and marked the end of rock with a conscience. They were everything rock was no longer supposed to be—self-destructive, whining, immature, dangerous, mean-spirited, bigoted and misogynist—and flaunting it all. Needless to say the media were on them like flies. This was the same attitude that heavy metal had started eight years ago, but Guns N' Roses had found a more acceptable-sounding musical formula, one that fit surprisingly well with the retro sounds on the charts at the time.

Interviewing these guys was a blast. Talking to Slash and Duffy in 1987 after the release of *Appetite for Destruction,* I gave Canada its first TV exposure to the lads. They were sniffling and visibly shaking throughout the interview. Self-conscious and defensive, they had come to expect tough interviews. No one wanted to talk about the music; their drug use was far more exciting stuff. They couldn't defend themselves, so they didn't try very hard. They had nothing to say about everything. Sullen and uncooperative—the teens were back in town.

G N' R were pivotal in the retaking of the music industry by teenage rock and roll. Without their success there would have been no Nirvana, no Pearl Jam, no grunge movement at all. We would all be listening to E.L.O. boxed sets for another ten years. For a while, Guns N' Roses seemed on the verge of successfully self-destructing but they pulled back at the last moment. Reportedly in therapy for everything that initially made them successful, the boys stopped just short of the leave a beautiful corpse syndrome. Guns N' Roses have been left behind, because their spirit crumbled, and because they broke the first commandment of rock: Thou shalt not "dis" thy fans. The petulant walk-offs and incredible delays during their 1992 tour—be it for sore throats, bad sound or whatever—left their audiences feeling insulted and angry, and ended with violent consequences. (Remember the riot scene in Montreal?) The behaviour the band should have saved for record company execs and journalists was used against the very teenagers who made them successful. Add to that the fact that their music is really not very inventive—too reminiscent of the 1960s (a decade more and more kids wish would disappear forever)—and you have a band that is on its way out.

The grunge movement from Seattle that has replaced G N' R still has a bad boy element, but the groups tend to be more focused, intelligent and less volatile. Bands like Soundgarden, Pearl Jam and Nirvana brought teen dispirit to top-ten radio, but in typical teen fashion, it's just about impossible to figure out what Kurt Cobain is singing in "Smells Like Teen Spirit." While abhorring politics in music, and much more low-key than hardcore, grunge musicians write realistically about their grimy world. Unlike heavy metal, which drew mostly on fantasy situations, the grunge world of Seattle is real, and the drug use, suicide and depression they write about is from experience. Taking a cue from The Boomtown Rats' "I Don't Like Mondays," Pearl Jam's "Jeremy" is as powerful a song as the 1990s could ask for, and perfectly in tune with its teen audience.

Recent press reports tell us that for nearly half of Canadian teens, fear plays a significant role in their daily lives. They are afraid of each other, afraid of roving gangs of teenagers and afraid of the disturbed kid in homeroom class that may just lose it one day. Eleven percent of our teens have been robbed or assaulted, and 11 percent carry knives for protection from other teens.

Despite those depressing statistics, the people who listen to grunge apparently hold a different world-view from the one expressed by the nihilistic bands from seedy Seattle. Polls show that 1990s Canadian teens are hopeful, driven and focused. They care about school, their families and the future, without being naive. The teen of the 1990s may be the most mature adolescent generation in a long time. Yet the musicians who represent them are not as together as the fans. A disturbing trend back to heroin use in the music scene is slowly picking off its brightest members. Mother Love Bone's singer Andrew Wood and the Red Hot Chili Peppers' guitarist Hillel Slovel both died before they got to see their music hit the mainstream, and rumours of Kurt Cobain and Courtney Love's heroin use while expecting their first child suggested a grotesque scene. While music fans in their thirties look at smack use and marvel that anyone could still be that stupid, they forget that heroin's reputation has changed. No longer the most dangerous of drugs, compared to crack, heroin looks like an organic, relatively safe alternative for those young enough not to have watched their musical heroes die from it.

Canadian grunge groups are just as teen-centred as the Seattle movement, but they tend to take themselves a lot less seriously than their American counterparts and they aren't grounded in a drug culture. Halifax's Sloan put Canadian grunge on the map, and their more tempered depression, while less exotic than the Seattle scene, may suit our mood more closely.

The 1992 Lollapalooza tour—the teenage rock event of the year—brought teens out in Toronto to see the one concert of the summer that was truly for them. But while the Red Hot Chili Peppers were doing their version of Neil Young's "The Needle and the Damage Done," the kids were lining up to buy all-natural high-energy drinks. To the audience of mostly middle-class Canadian kids (with the exception of the requisite number of acid astronauts), the heroin references on stage seemed more a case of self-therapy than preaching to the masses. But in our cities, heroin use is soaring, and health agencies across the country have been caught by surprise. As the recession continues, teens are forgotten, exploited and discouraged, and health experts are predicting a heroin epidemic could soon hit Canadian middle- and upper-class teenagers the way it already has in Europe and the United States.

While heroin use is just plain stupid, I can understand where the instinct is coming from. Young people are trying to completely rebuild the counterculture—a scene that almost disappeared in the affluent 1980s—and, like the bra-burning feminists of the 1960s, they have to come out of the gate running. This time around, the pop world was in such dire need of a major fix that it prematurely shoved the newly formed grunge movement into the spotlight as the new messiah.

Whether or not grunge can hold centrestage remains to be seen. The odds are against it. But in the meantime, rock and roll has gone back to the people that started it all—teenagers. And what fun to think that the music industry, now a mega corporate concern, is at the mercy of a teenage population of consumers. Reminds me of the scene in The Beatles' *A Hard Day's Night* in which the advertising executives are trying desperately to clue in to the teenage fashion psyche. In twenty-five years, rock has come full circle.

# whispering pines

in which we learn how to whistle
in the woods to keep our spirits up

In thinking about Canadian culture, I keep coming back to two or three things that Northrop Frye had to say about the subject. First, that our regionalism is one of the big strengths of Canadian artists, and second, that the Big Question facing Canadian artists today is not "Who am I?"—the one that stumps the Yanks and the Brits—but rather, "Where is Here?"

I know that Frye would sit late at night in his North Toronto house picking out Haydn on his piano, but I have no idea what his views on Canadian popular music might have been. I'd bet the farm, however, that Frye's views on Canadian literature apply equally well to Canadian pop, and to most other aspects of Canadian culture.

I want to discuss both regionalism and identity as they relate to Canadian pop and rock music, and add into the mix—if it's not too audacious to tack on a little something to Norrie's list—the idea of the "removed voice." The fact that we're still sitting here at the southern fringe of a great frontier, having managed to slip the British yoke and not entirely replace it with the American one, is what gives us a perspective and a voice. And from out here in Frye's "bush garden," that removed voice is growing increasingly persuasive and is more and more being heard.

## finding our voice

In an essay in his collection *Divisions on a Ground,* Frye argues that over the course of the 1800s, Canadian literature moved from being an expression of a provincial outpost of imperial Britain to taking on a real and legitimate voice of its own. That is, people writing in Canada first tended to write about the fact that they were not someplace else—usually not in their bucolic childhood homes in pastoral England. In both content and style, they were essentially colonial; they defined themselves by where they were not. By the time Prime Minister Wilfrid Laurier announced that the twentieth century would belong to Canada, however, Canadian artists were happier owning up to their home, which was even, in some cases, their birthplace. Frontier references about bleak, wintry landscapes were yielding to revels in the romance of space, distance and high tides at Grand Pré. By the end of World War I, Canadian painters had left the silly, pseudo-pre-

Raphaelite style of Homer Watson's Gothic boatman on the Styx; instead, Lawren Harris was moving towards the increasingly powerful and modernist mountainscapes of the Canadian Shield and points west. They had found their place, their style, their voice. It was removed from and remote from that of their British forebears and American cousins.

I think that much the same kind of development has happened in Canadian music. That is, for a great deal of its recorded development, which has only been of any significance since World War II, Canadian popular music was either a pale imitation of the British music hall, or a reflection of the brilliance of the Brill Building in New York City. However, in the last twenty years, Canadian popular musicians have found a voice. As it turns out, perhaps not surprisingly, that voice has tended to be folk-inspired and often rural, most lately manifesting itself in country music and, even more recently, in country music performed by women.

I want to argue that what has emerged in the last twenty years in Canada could not have emerged in the United States, and that there is something distinct about Canadian rural and regional roots that our American neighbours don't share. Now at first this seems counter-intuitive; after all, culture doesn't respect political boundaries, and traditional oral cultures (such as folk music) prefer to follow trade routes, watersheds, communication and transportation links. And we know that most of the natural trading routes in North America are north-south. So how can there be any solely Canadian regions that would give rise to a peculiar and distinct "removed voice"? Aren't Halifax and Bangor, Maine, interchangeable, and isn't Winnipeg just Des Moines North?

No. Whether it's because there is still a frontier in the Canadian consciousness that has faded from the American mind, or because oral culture carries greater importance in less densely populated, more rural cultures; whether there is less capital for technological advances in the infrastructures of transportation and communications, or less discretionary income for homeowners to spend on new communications technology; whether it's because of an insistence on our idea of the "mosaic"; whether it's because our music is simply not being made in the United States, or whether any of this has anything to do with it—the fact of the matter is that there is a more removed voice in Canadian music. What is it removed from? From the centre of popular music, which originates from the industrially inspired towers of New York, Nashville, Memphis, Chicago and Los Angeles.

Regionalism has continued to inform Canadian popular music in a way that has largely been lost in the States. The music made in Detroit or Philadelphia may be predominantly of one genre or another, depending on the cultural mix in the city at the time, but it will not always be different from the music of that genre made in L.A., Chicago or New York. If there are differences between, say, heavy metal from L.A. and heavy metal from Chicago, these will have very little to do with the region from which each emanates. The surfeit of pop music in the United States and the homogeneity of the record companies and radio-programming process have removed much of the regional flavour in American popular music from all but very specialized record stores.

This is not so true in the Canadian case. It would be tempting to say that the traditional philosophy of the Canadian "mosaic" has been friendlier to regional differences that the American "melting pot." More likely, Canadian content regulations requiring a certain percentage of domestic music in radio programming have meant that musicians who have not had the edges rounded off their regional backgrounds make it to Canadian airwaves. The history of Canadian culture is also inextricably linked to the advantage of having a state-owned broadcasting system, the CBC, with a mandate to promote regionalism on both radio and TV. To some extent, this has meant that artists in Canada, while they do not become stars and rarely become wealthy, nevertheless do get heard.

Let us take as an example—and an outstanding one at that—the experience of Canadian songwriter and singer Stan Rogers. Rogers's rich baritone, his social activism and his Maritime resonances meant that he received exposure on Canadian airways in a way that is unlikely to have happened in the States, where even established artists working in a similar style, like Pete Seeger, are very rarely heard outside of the most specialized programs or tributes.

## the roots of the canadian sound

In the beginning of non-aboriginal original North American music, there was folk singing. It was accompanied by the technology of portable music of the day: stringed instruments, like fiddles, viols, bass fiddles, mandolins and guitars; sometimes squeezeboxes and accordions (but not pianos—that was parlour music, much later). Guitars became favoured because the singer could accompany himself with a fairly rich range of chords. The folk music clan that married bluegrass to Appalachian begat country. The folk music that married gospel to blues (black folk music) begat rock and roll. Jazz is from somewhere else—Africa, via New Orleans, St. Louis and Chicago. So, in this essay, I see acoustic folk music as a direct ancestor of both country and rock and roll music—guitar-based, verse/chorus/verse in structure.

For most of its brief, thirty-year history, rock music has been only rarely Canadian, even when some of the best of it was being made by Canadians. Even when Burton Cummings and the Guess Who in the early 1970s addressed the issue head on in "American Woman," the sound and impact of the music were at heart American. (It is interesting that Cummings's band-mate in the Guess Who, Randy Bachman, attained what is, in my view, a more remote or un-American pop sound with his next band, Bachman Turner Overdrive, and particularly with their jazz-influenced "Blue Collar" and anthemic "Taking Care of Business," the latter being remade much later by Vancouver's DOA as a vehicle for a music video featuring a frenzied hockey match.)

More notably remote, and certainly more influential, were Joni Mitchell and Neil Young. While they both started out writing and singing folk songs, their music today has evolved into jazz-folk in Joni Mitchell's case, and rock and roll for Neil Young. Both wrote early folk songs featuring the Canadian landscape. Both, even in their later, successful careers, have been iconoclasts, with a sense of apartness, of not belonging to the pop mainstream. As for Mitchell, her early years in Saskatchewan must have something to do with that. Mitchell's swooping vocalizations and rhythmically dense jazz tendencies have surfaced in the music of both Jane Siberry and Vancouver singer Mae Moore. While Siberry uses reductionist technique to give her lyrics a kind of primitive or naive flair, set against a fairly sophisticated musical texture, it isn't spun like something you'd hear on a New York psychiatrist's couch: the images are often rural or domestic.

Whatever the case to be made for Mitchell's distinctive Canadian sound, I feel more comfortable making the claim for Neil Young, even though, like Mitchell, he is clearly and permanently transplanted to California, although he spent a good deal of time in "a town in North Ontario." Nevertheless, Young continues to put out classic rock and roll that is rooted in many of the same folk tendencies as that of Mitchell—strong structures, an emphasis on lyrics even in the heaviest of tunes, the use of the guitar as basis for rhythm and melody. These elements provide a direct link to the scene where they both got their start, the Riverboat coffee house on Yorkville Avenue in Toronto, in the 1960s.

It's not just coincidence that the potent folk scene of New York in the early 1960s manifested itself only months later in the Yorkville scene in Toronto. This was in part a political movement, in that American draft-resisters found Toronto a friendly, familiar and safe haven. And with only five hundred miles between Toronto and New York—at the most a day and a half's hitch-hike—Toronto people were also familiar with the Bleecker Street folk scene. So it was that Canadians such as Ian and Sylvia Tyson and Gordon Lightfoot were within a folk tradition whose biggest stars lived in New York. So, in spite of the fact that all the necessities of a burgeoning folk scene were already well in place in Canada, it was the legitimizing influence of the New York scene that gave rise to the Riverboat. In typically Canadian fashion, it could not happen commercially until good evidence from Gerde's Folk City and the Bottom Line in New York relieved the trepidations of risk-averse Canadian investors.

The fact that folk music is essentially acoustic guitar based was a key ingredient to the ruralness of the sound. It meant that the instrument of composition was available to the junior composer with limited means, and a long distance between band-mates. It was a solitary medium, and nothing suited the long rural spaces in Canada better that that.

Writing about regional voices within Canadian popular music, one must say something about the music of Quebec. As is often the case, the cultural scene in Quebec has a different background and doesn't quite fit the thesis I've developed to discuss English-speaking Canada. However, an interesting point can be made through a discussion of one seminal Quebec-based artist, Leonard Cohen.

Like novelist Mordecai Richler, Cohen's region and tradition are those of Montreal's vibrant Jewish community. A respected poet and novelist in the early 1960s, Cohen was impressed by the success of Bob Dylan's tantalizingly obscure lyrics, rudimentary chording and instrumentation and peculiar vocal stylings, and decided that the mid-1960s presented an unusual opportunity for the setting of poetry to music. Unlike Dylan, Cohen cannot sing (want to fight about it?), but his drone is infectious, like waking up to a truck outside your window on a sub-zero Montreal morning, the engine trying hard to turn over, the lethargic motor grinding ceaselessly. At other times, one can hear strains of the Hebrew cantor, or the growl of Greenwich Village bohemians of the Kerouac and Kesey era. Early classics like "Suzanne," with its love-generation morality and psychedelic amoebalike slide shows, now seem dated. The later songs, like "First We'll Take Manhattan," are more pointed, lonely, acerbic and timely. While Cohen borrowed heavily from Dylan and others of the New York rock intelligentsia, especially the Velvet Underground, his voice remains a distinctly regional Canadian one. It is interesting to speculate about how much Cohen's approach has influenced the sound of Toronto's Cowboy Junkies, whose style offers much of the same slow, deliberate, reductionist dirge and drone.

So much has been written and said about Gordon Lightfoot's Canadianism that I think we can take it as given. Although I don't listen to a lot of Lightfoot, I attend his Toronto concerts every year, and every year I get the same magic feeling of being part of an audience that is completely in tune with the performer, and vice versa. We're a weepy lot, Lightfoot audiences, and he is consistently able to pull our common chords. Lightfoot is very important to this argument for two reasons: he is a recognizably Canadian voice, and he didn't move to L.A.! He is the key to why so much Canadian music has been received in the States as country music. After his twelve-string period of the 1960s, Lightfoot introduced a slide steel guitar into the mix, and to the limited mind of the American radio programmer, that was the sound of country music. Most of his later work—"Daylight Katie," "Alberta Bound," etc.—mainly appeared on country charts. Lightfoot has always had a clear sense of place and has never been embarrassed to strut it lyrically—even when other popular musicians were trying hard to disguise their Canadian roots.

The group that took the Riverboat-era folk roots and soaked them in Arkansas country-rock was the increasingly influential, The Band. Though assembled originally to support that Svengali of Canadian rock, Ronnie Hawkins, a transplanted Elvis clone, its distinctive Canadian voice soon emerged. Four of the band were from southern Ontario and brought with them an eclectic mix of regional sounds of the 1950s. Keyboardist Garth Hudson carried with him the influence of small-town Anglican church organ music. Robbie Robertson, lead guitarist and writer, who joined up with Hawkins as a roadie, grew up near the Mohawk Six Nations reserve near Brantford, Ontario, the home of his grandmother. The other two members were Toronto session players, Richard Manuel and Rick Danko. Transplanted to Woodstock, New York, as a house band for a recuperating Bob Dylan, fresh from a tumble on his Triumph Bonneville, The Band developed their music around Robbie Robertson's poetic lyrics.

This band sounded like no other, in part because of the remote voice they brought with them. Levon Helm's American voice, no doubt, is associated with that of Dixie rebels—a lost but authentic American voice that was no longer part of the mainstream, and one with curious affinities to a rural Canadian experience. Listen carefully, though, to songs like "Whispering Pines" ("Drifting in a daze / when evenings will be done / try looking through a haze / at an empty house in the cold, cold sun") or, more pointedly, "Acadian Driftwood," a song about the expulsion of French Acadians from Nova Scotia, which nicely marries the Québécois fiddle to the Cajun music of New Orleans and contains the lyric "I've got winter in my blood." Even after a long hiatus, Robertson's solo work has tended to centre on his aboriginal roots, and, despite the claims of aboriginal spokespeople that white borders are meaningless, I would still argue that his voice is essentially remote and rural, and therefore traceable to Canadian regional influences.

The Band, with its original lineup, expired in the mid-1970s and in the early 1980s another kind of Canadian music was making money in the States. Loverboy, The Spoons, Honeymoon Suite and Saga were bona fide rock stars. These people, in contrast to

The Band, had no Canadian voice at all; they were made to fit the American formula. Since there was nothing distinctive about them, they only really attained star status in Canada once they'd been confirmed as authentic south of the border, thereby reinforcing the cliché "Canada eats its young." This posing as American rock stars soon became as obvious to the Canadian fan as a faked injury in an NHL game. These bands soon, and appropriately, withered.

On the folk end of things, Bruce Cockburn established himself as an artist of tremendous international reputation mainly because of his anti-American politics. But you can't decry U.S. involvement in Central America and expect to get a lot of U.S. airplay, so Cockburn's attraction was mostly in Japan and Europe. And, unlike the pop stars of the day, Cockburn, like Lightfoot, had no qualms talking about "Where is Here?" in his lyrics.

## hometown heroes

By the early 1980s, the holy grail of a U.S. chart hit no longer had the hip appeal to Canadian artists. It was seen as a sell-out; it was also so difficult to get that it was hardly worth working for. The success of independent groups and labels in the United States and Britain showed us another route. Canada went underground. We gave ourselves the luxury of time, cut ourselves off from the *Billboard* bullets and looked for what felt right, and ours—not theirs. We were trying to find out "Where is Here?" and we were ready to develop our own industry. Musicians seemed content to stay in their basements longer. What was now important was developing a hometown audience.

By the second half of the decade, groups like the Northern Pikes, Grapes of Wrath and Blue Rodeo stole power from the multinational record companies and put it back into the hands of the fans. In a desperate bid to stay hip, record companies were forced to drive down to warehouse rehearsal spaces to sign bands in an effort to capitalize on the underground swell. Canadian music benefited. Those artists who deserved them got record deals. They had already released their own product independently, and maybe even had their own video. They were better rehearsed. They were more likely to get on tape what they wanted musically. While the sound and production were rough, it was different and more like our own. Producers like Daniel Lanois and Michael Philip Wojewoda were kept busy here at home. While those early records all sounded the same—too full, too busy, too little separation and space—Canadians were able to listen beyond the problems of first studio efforts and were rewarded with music that no one anywhere else was producing.

The self-consciousness of Loverboy rock was gone. There was a new confidence. The hip quotient was now in being from someplace else—the satisfaction of a joke that middle America couldn't get. In the face of this positive attitude, punk didn't really catch on big in Canada. Its tunelessness was somehow imported, and there were no genuine street politics to go along with it. Queen Street in Toronto launched into its black-hennaed, Doc Martened phase that survives today.

Useful bands such as Rough Trade attempted to speak to an increasingly political gay and lesbian audience, as did Parachute Club. Both made fine urban music but found limited commercial appeal.

One of the most influential of the new voices on Toronto's Queen Street was Handsome Ned, who, since the early 1980s, led a kind of urban country band and whose death by heroin overdose in 1987 was a key marshalling point for the blossoming cow-punk community. It seemed that only through his death did the urban-country bands in the city realize they were part of a very potent scene. By 1986, the revitalized Horseshoe Tavern had ended its aimless association with punk and new music and returned to a more focused country policy. Among the most influential of the bands who began to play under that policy was Blue Rodeo, who have achieved major crossover radio play with melodically and lyrically strong country-rock songs. At the same time, the Northern Pikes, a band with a distinctive country-rock voice from Saskatoon, were putting the Prairies on the musical map and touring successfully across the country.

While the sound was country, its roots were folk. Even with the advent of synthesizers, the basis of the music was still the acoustic guitar, and the song structure still that of the folk song. And while the musicians were definitely urban, their roots were rural—after all, Toronto, for a lot of people, is simply a place where you find work, not necessarily where you come from. So the earlier, folksy roots of Canadian popular music matured into a much more countrified sound—a sound that could be heard even in the hard-edged rock of bands like the Northern Pikes or the alternative sounds of the new female artists from across the country.

## women's work

The other main voice in Toronto that emerged in the late 1980s is that of women singers, who offer a different sensibility easily accommodated within the country form. The Cowboy Junkies provide, perhaps, the best example. Highlighting singer Margo Timmins's mournful voice, the Cowboy Junkies first achieved cult status and then wide popular acceptance with their valium-laced approach. Musically infantile arrangements did not impede their impact since they were tapping into the kind of languid melancholy that country music has often traded in. If you listen to Timmins's a cappella version of "Mining for Gold" on their *Trinity Sessions* album, however, the hipness of country hurt becomes very evident.

Less prominent, but still well within the range, is Mary Margaret O'Hara, who has a long history with Toronto bands. O'Hara's long auburn hair and scattered, epileptic style make her a kind of ultra-hip gloss on Sissy Spacek as Loretta Lynn. There is no better example of the hybrid between straight-ahead country and the truly alternative Toronto scene than Mary Margaret's music. Unfortunately, she had to go to Britain to get a decent record deal. Never sacrificing poetry or musical prowess, she manages to keep the best intentions of country music without ever sounding like anyone else in the business. O'Hara's hiccuppy voice can belt out a song with force, and, on a barn-burner like "Brand New Day" on her debut album, the country influence is unmistakable.

Probably no other force has done more for the mainstreaming of new country music as the authoritative Canadian voice than k.d. lang, whose widely acclaimed talent has deservedly met with major success around the world. While singing country, lang set the standard. She was able to modernize country without belittling it. While she certainly used parody in her stage show (along with all kinds of things she had learned as a performance artist), her love of the music rang out loud and clear; for many of us in her urban audience, she legitimized pure country music. She swung from a kind of goofy, galumphing style to a very sophisticated style all her own. Again, like Cockburn, her politics impeded her progress: her outspoken stand against eating meat did not open many doors in middle America or western Canadian country radio stations, and rumours of her sexual preferences—now out in the open—turned away the Nashville set.

While she certainly was noticed, k.d. never had a bona fide hit singing country. Happily, her non-hit status is all behind her now, but in her swing away from country, lang is still offering us a distinct regional voice—the influence of the western Ukrainian contingent is easily picked up in Ben Mink's arrangements—and while she may be now labelled "adult contemporary," there is an isolation and remoteness that she draws from again and again.

There are many other examples to demonstrate the

sweep of Canadian popular music towards country music, and female country music at that. Michelle Wright is Canada's biggest country star at the moment, while on the folkier end of country, Mae Moore, Meryn Cadell and Sarah McLachlan are gaining North American acceptance. An earlier generation of male country singers is also maintaining a strong following. Ian Tyson's authentic singing cowboy approach remains a true regional voice of the west, while Stompin' Tom Connors, with his broadly nationalistic songs about Canada and her characters, consistently gathers new young fans.

## going to country

If this is the trend, then what are its implications? Country music is, after all, essentially American, a borrowed form. Why have young Canadian artists—often urban, young, female Canadians—adopted it as their own, and how is the result different from the American product?

One of the attractions of country music as a form is that it is unashamed to be emotionally raw. Between the periods of sophistication (Hank Williams Sr. and now some of the newer artists) came an awful lot of hurtin' housewife music in which blonde-bouffanted singers outdid each other to see who could sing more personally about their lives. It was sung gossip along the "loved, abused and left" theme. Women were appendages, and happy to cast themselves that way. The new country music has jettisoned that point of view and replaced it with a more ironic and relevant one. A second major attraction of the form is that it is musically simplistic and therefore broadly available to both players and audiences. There is a danger here, however; in its simplicity, it can expose a bad band, since there is less to hide behind—less instrumentation, less volume and less density.

Canadian country music has a twang to it, but that twang is not the classic Southern drawl but more the dropped "g"s and the irony of the concession roads. It is intelligent, not in the kind of self-conscious smartness of a Mark Twain or a Will Rogers, but in that kind of way that comes from looking at things all round, from the outside, from some other place. And if that's the Canadian voice, how is it heard, particularly in the vast, yawning market to the south, the home of country music?

First, let's get literal. What does the Canadian voice sound like? The Canadian accent is highly regarded in the United States. Peter Jennings and J.D. Roberts didn't get to be anchors because of their highly regional patois. The Canadian accent is considered neutral but authoritative. It has, I suspect, enough residual Britishness to American ears to conjure up a faint memory of its older relatives.

And in many ways, the sound of that voice has important connections to American country music. Linguists have argued that perhaps the closest accent to lower-class seventeenth-century British accents can be found in the Appalachian hills, where early English settlers to Virginia moved shortly after their arrival on this side of the big splash. There they quickly achieved inbred isolation and managed to capture that accent in time, while they diminished the gene pool. And of course that hillbilly accent has ascended through bluegrass folk songs to American country music today. In the sound of the Canadian voice, there may be a resonance to Americans, since we also sound somewhat British, dated and antique to their ears.

There is a more important aspect, however, to the way the Canadian voice is heard in the American market. To understand it, we should look at a parallel situation involving two other countries in the early part of this century: Ireland and England. Between 1890 and 1930, much of the world's best literature in English wasn't written in England but in Ireland, or at least by Irish writers. Consider the list: Oscar Wilde, George Bernard Shaw, W.B. Yeats, James Joyce, Sean O'Casey, Samuel Beckett. This happened after two centuries of political, cultural and economic imperialism of the worst kind, a foreign policy that bordered at one point on genocide. But by the end of that horrible century, Irish writers were setting the standard for English literature.

In that forty-year period, the Irish voice achieved an ascendancy. The voice was from a country that spoke English (after its own language was outlawed) extraordinarily well, but was very different—it was Catholic, mystical, poor, nationalistic and angry. Shaw's wordy journalistic commentary on British morality, Wilde's cutting satire of English society, Yeats's nationalism, Joyce's global comedy in his recreation of Dublin from exile—they all depend on a perspective that is non-

English, and yet in English (or with Joyce, at least a kind of English!).

And so it is, or will be soon, with the Canadian voice. Canadians have been dominated by more subtle, but no less powerful, imperial influences: before World War II by the British, and since by the United States. And as we come to the end of this century, the Canadian voice will achieve, from our unique and removed perspective, an authority and an ascendancy. Its remoteness to the American audience is clear. Especially in Quebec. In many ways, Quebec is far ahead of English-speaking Canada in the quest for self-realization.

## the song remains the same

Like any industrial or economic commodity in Canada, once it has been reduced to a mere financial commodity, music will follow natural trading lines. The natural business linkages for Canadian music and most other commercial goods are north-south, not east-west. But that's nothing new. The first Canadians knew the only way to battle that geographic reality was to carve a railway through the north-south barriers and create this artificial country of whistlestop towns along the U.S. border. While political boundaries have always been mainly artificial, they can be defended. Airwaves can't. Canadian radios picked up far more American stations than Canadian ones.

And yet that situation has brought with it its own backlash, an inherent demise. For all its sheer artificiality, our country has within it, I think, a kind of constant search for identity, a creativity in answering the question "Where is Here?" Of course, this identity is easier to define negatively, as what it is not, and what it has traditionally not been is American. In the 1950s, people knew what hockey announcer Foster Hewitt meant when he opened every "Hockey Night in Canada" broadcast with "Hello Canada and hockey fans in the United States." What he meant was "All Canada is of course listening to this hockey game, and a few sturdy souls in the soulless U.S. probably have enough good sense to come to appreciate this northern game too." It sets us apart. Canadian music in the 1980s finally had enough momentum to make its crucial breakaway from the overpowering American sound.

How does the Canadian government, which once made a bit of a show of supporting cultural industries, see the Canadian music industry now? Our trade linkages, which have always been anti-Canadian by geography, are now anti-Canadian by the official free trade policy of the Canadian government. Large multinational record companies will be unlikely to see Toronto as the regional headquarters of the north-east or central Midwest; surely New York, Boston, Detroit and Chicago, all within five hundred miles of various sections of the Canadian market, will be preferred. In ten years, with the full application of the current free trade policy, I doubt that any multinational record distributor will choose to locate a major office in Toronto, Montreal or Vancouver. We'll simply be commercial outposts in the vast, suburban, American market.

And paradoxically, that could be beneficial to Canadian music. While substantial Canadian sales await, in the North American market Canadian music will achieve cult status. And cult status has always been accorded good music on the leading edge. Having to sell ourselves to the multinationals down south to get a decent record deal will have the effect of making fewer Canadian rock stars rich, but at the same time will make more Canadian popular music of genuine regional value. Ironically, Canadian music might achieve the status enjoyed by Australian films today or by Irish literature in the early part of this century, thus making it even more attractive to an American audience. (Early in 1994, Toronto's Colin Linden made Canadian music history with two of his songs in the top ten on two different charts. One song written for The Band hit the pop top ten, and another for Michelle Wright in the country charts.)

In an effort to engender a feeling of national unity, Canada has had to take extreme measures: a national railroad, a national radio service, a national TV service and Canadian content quotas. But the railroads sit rusting, and free trade may erode what's left of many of our cultural institutions. Yet it is exactly at this precarious moment that Canadian music will find its true voice. A new confidence, gained from international recognition on our own terms, is the start of a new movement in Canadian music. "Here" is where we are, and we like it. We know what we're not, and we're not "There."

Canadians have lost faith in their politicians to pull the country together and are naturally turning to other ways to identify themselves and think about themselves with value. Whether you're sitting on the docks in Lunenburg, Nova Scotia, with the wives of the trawler fishermen waiting for the boats to come in after their fourteen-day stint on the Grand Banks, or driving through the foothills of the Rockies in a half-ton looking for a stray steer, the music on the truck radios will be country music. Outside Toronto, country music is everywhere, and, even in Toronto, it's available on two radio stations all the time.

In the 1980s, our urban country music was mainly recorded in Toronto, and it was the sound of Toronto recognizing that it is merely the place where people from across Canada have gathered to make money. In the 1990s, it is no longer necessary to travel to Toronto to create top-quality recordings; music is being made all over the country. Our Canadian music is a maturing form, and one to which large numbers of people turn to hear resonances of where they come from, of their regional pasts, blended with the cosmopolitanism of where they are now. It is a commentary on the American form which in many ways it has improved upon, and which it is ready to take to new places in the years to come.

In this sad moment of our history, with the country seemingly adrift, Canadians are having to turn to the one thread of identity we have left, and that identity is found in the arts. Even some in government have realized that the only hope for pulling this country back together again lies in our collective vision of ourselves as expressed in the arts. The 1992 "Citizens' Forum on Canada's Future" wanted our destiny articulated by poets rather than politicians and lawyers. I would call that real progress. Our new national identity will be built on a strong base, and a maturing regional voice will be there to sing it out. As remote as our songs may have been, they are getting close to the heart of things, and it is at the heart of things that country music is most often found.

# rogues' gallery

in which we learn the innermost thoughts of famous men, maybe

## lou reed

Lou Reed is an ugly, ugly guy. He has bad hair, bad skin and a bad attitude. He arrives in a big, black limousine. His wife is his manager and she opens the door for him and takes his overcoat. Lou is wearing a very expensive leather suit jacket. It is brand new and very black. He says "Don't try to pin that microphone on my new, very expensive jacket." Instead we pin it on his very black turtleneck sweater.

Lou has a new, totally black piece of vinyl out. It's about sitting on hypodermic needles on Coney Island beach. It's about how New York is an awful place. Lou loves New York. This record is Lou's version of the "I Love New York" commercials. (*And the coloured girls go...*)

Lou takes a long time to say little. He keeps his voice real low so I have to lean way in on him to hear anything. He keeps talking about his guitar. I don't care about his guitar. I want to find out why music doesn't satisfy him. He won't answer me.

His wife, manager, door-opener and coat-holder says it's time to go to the airport. Lou gets up and waits for his overcoat to be put over his shoulders. Liberace meets Darth Vader. I say goodbye and I can't wait for the Lou Reed album of Christmas favourites. He looks at me like I just said I can't wait for the Lou Reed album of Christmas favourites. He gets into his big, black car. His wife shuts the door and sits up front with the driver. Then the car explodes in a million tiny, black bits.

## iggy pop

**I**ggy Pop is trying to outlive the guy on the Alpha-Getti can. They may be the same person—he's not sure. Iggy's little and dangerous, but he's not what he calls sexy. It bugs him. Sometimes he thinks he'd like to be like Bowie, suave-like. Get spreads in *GQ* magazine, get to wear loafers and nice sweaters. But no go. Iggy's wardrobe has been the same for twenty years: black T-shirt, black jeans, black leather jacket, black running shoes. Iggy has faced the fact that he is still a teenager, even though he's forty-six, now married, has just got his first chequebook and has some money in the account, too. Iggy doesn't want to take life too fast. *GQ* will bang his door down at sixty. (Hopefully then, Alpha-Getti will be out of business and Bowie won't look so great any more.)

## daniel lanois' neighbourhood

Daniel Lanois answers the knock at the door. It's his new friends who have come to make a recording of their music in his house. He says, "Welcome, come in!" and invites this new band to change into their sneakers and put some comfortable sweaters on. He explains to his friend the engineer that his new friends have some new songs they would like to play for him and could he please roll the tape. Daniel closes the window, saying "I don't want to make too much noise in the neighbourhood," and takes his place behind the coffee table console. Although he doesn't say it out loud, Daniel thinks their music is too jangly, it's not smooth, but the music makes him see some beautiful pictures in his head, and using a paper plate, construction paper, glue and paints, he shows the band what he sees. The band agrees it's beautiful and Daniel agrees to make the band sound like his picture. They all co-operate and share and have fun without disturbing the neighbours.

## david byrne

When someone told him his picture was on the cover of *Time* magazine, David Byrne was relieved. For the first time he felt that he fit in somewhere, and if his face was going to be on the cover, he couldn't really be too weird-looking.

His paper face was getting a coffee-table view of America, and David Byrne could navigate those sharp corners with his eyes shut; that's what got him on the cover of *Time*.

He sat in his own house contemplating all those faces on all those coffee tables. There were round tables, square ones, wooden ones, glass ones, matching little ones at either ends of plastic-covered couches—he knew more about the tables than he knew about the big face on the magazine cover.

David got off his couch and, avoiding the coffee table, walked to the TV and turned it on. The picture came to life, he hugged the TV: he loved the warmth of this machine and he felt sure he could actually feel the light waves penetrating into his chest. He never changed the channel; he had grown to like whichever one was on now. He knew it, it was TV he could trust.

He'd have to go outside soon, but for now he just sat on his couch and listened to the noises of the house and the voices on the TV. How had he managed to go so far when most of the time his head felt so blank? Would people stare at the cover of *Time*, would they figure out that those pinhole Orphan Annie eyes that give off no clues also take nothing in? David Byrne is blind—blind, blind, blind, blind, blind.

## miles davis

Miles Davis is a very clean person. He instructs all of his visitors to leave their shoes outside his apartment, just like the Japanese do. His apartment looks Japanese, too—rice-paper screens over the windows, and not much furniture. Miles Davis knows he is the coolest person alive. In fact, he's surprised he's alive. That his body is such a burden makes him cool against all odds. Not only does his body sometimes let him down, but his brain does, too. What is this girl saying? What was the question? Never mind, keep talking—talk about music. Play her some Prince—we're very much alike. Prince has written a letter. "Hang out with me," it says. "It will make you famous." It just might. Two little black cool men sizing each other up. That appeals. He can't think of anything else to say. He runs his fingers over his chest for the hundredth time that hour. Touching his skin reminds him he's still alive and still feeling too much. Worn-smooth like worry beads, his skin is very much a part of the fragile cool of Miles Davis.

## johnny lydon

Johnny Lydon is deliriously happy. He's in love, he's got a lot of money, and he's just made another record that makes him feel wonderful.

As he lunges into another chair in yet another hotel room for yet another interview, he can feel the expectations of the interviewer suck all the positive energy out of him. The sad truth is, Lydon has been playing a role he hasn't wanted to play for a long, long time. The one person who never gave a shit is now forced to never give a shit. The Peter Pan of rock and roll runs around giving people exactly what they want, exactly what they still need—a blast of obnoxious, self-centred adolescent rage. It seems to have the same effect as confession. The interviewers seem to leave slightly shaken, but feeling better about themselves for going through with it and surviving—a badge of honour. He thinks of a better metaphor—Ernest Angley, that fat slap of benediction on the forehead. Picking up his beer, Johnny smiles and swallows again.

## robert plant

Robert Plant knows he's being watched closely. Not just by the interviewer or the cameraman, not only by the thousands of people (more, he hopes) that are tuned in right now, but by a keen inner eye that scrutinizes his every move. The line between cool and contrived is a very fine one, and looking down at his metal-tipped cowboy boots, he thinks he's picked the right boots.

Led Zeppelin knew a lot about rock and roll. What they didn't know, they invented—and it worked. Since their demise (well, it doesn't seem like Zeppelin ever ended—they were no limited time offer), Robert Plant's confidence is not what it should be. With half the rock bands today taking Zeppelin as their own to pillage freely, why shouldn't he come back and dish out new material? Why shouldn't he have the major corporate sponsorship deal with Coke? Why can't he cash in on the new rock and roll money? He deserves it. But no one wants to hear the new music, the stories of life on the road this week. They want the legend of twenty years ago, something he no longer is. He tries to play along, but inside he cringes at every premeditated slouch and toss of his hair. Leaving the interview he realizes that he has betrayed himself and his new music.

It's so different this time around. He doesn't remember the tightrope being so high, and his inner eye is starting to give him trouble. It's spending too much time amazed at how closely everyone is watching him. Too close. Too hot, too high. He pictures himself falling. The cowboy boots may have been a mistake.

## bryan ferry

His latest spread in *Vogue* makes Bryan Ferry uncomfortable. The hair is perfectly tossed around; his eyes are narrowed precisely to project the passion and intelligence that somehow thrives inside this lolling, lazy body. His tie is off-centre just enough to ensure he's not like anything else you're likely to find in a suit. All in all it's a great picture, but it's not him. His wife Lucy said "Very nice" but laughed when she saw the pictures. Bryan can never take himself that seriously—neither can Lucy. Last month she told a magazine that a toasted bacon-and-egg sandwich was better than sex. And he agrees. But remarks like that won't be the downfall of the mighty King of Suave, a title he has held for the last twenty years. His undoing will be his addiction. Too bad it isn't drugs, alcohol or women—that would bolster his image. But no, it's Stim-u-Dents, those barbaric-looking orange sticks used to stimulate your gums and pick your teeth. Look, there are fifteen of the little monsters sitting in the ash-tray beside the magazine. He's been careful to hide them when cameras are around, but lately he's been forgetful. He's just waiting for a picture to show up in some magazine of him digging around in his mouth with his little orange spear. He vows again to give them up. Not cold turkey, that would be impossible, but *Vogue* wouldn't accept an orange toothpick in the mouth. He's sure about that.

## gene simmons

**g**ene Simmons may well be The Ugliest Man in Rock and Roll Today. He knows it, too, but would dissolve if anyone ever actually said it to his face. All that would be left would be a large lump of soggy black leather and a few strands of heavily shellacked black hair. But put him onstage, give him a lot of smoke and fire, and he's the most powerful, confident, rock god around. His music is power; his sexual exploits are about power; his money is power. It's not the music, the sex or the money that he's in the business for—it's the power. What does rock wizard Gene Simmons need all that power for? He's done virtually nothing with it. That's because he needs every inch of its dazzling veil to distract us from noticing that he's The Ugliest Man in Rock and Roll Today. Gene Simmons has gone to fantastic lengths to avoid ridicule. All his blow and show is really saying "Pay no attention to that man behind the curtain." All it will take is for some young, brave girl to come along and tell him the truth about himself, and Gene Simmons and all his archaic rock posturing will vanish into thin air. Poof.

# the story so far

**i**n which we explain
ourselves and say goodbye

## songs to live by

**e**very one of us has a musical history. It doesn't matter whether we can sing a note, we all carry with us the pop music of our time. When children of the rock world get together, a quick survey of musical tastes is all it takes to tell who and what they're dealing with. So I present my own early musical history for your scrutiny.

1964. I remember staying up late in my pyjamas with my sister Susan in the basement to watch Ed Sullivan (while Mom did the ironing). The Beatles were on, and I remember asking Mom and Dad if it was all right to scream. They said yes, so with more than just a little self-consciousness, we did.

1966. The year I was allowed to have a record player in my room. My first album was a Christmas present from my parents—the first Monkees album. (It came with a list of rules dictating when and when not to play it, how loud and how long.) Favourite Monkee, Michael Nesmith. (I figured he was the ugliest, and I'd have a better chance of actually marrying him.)

1966. Formed the Ocelots with Jane Doner. We were two slinky seven-year-olds who wanted to be the Supremes. We practised every recess. We sang Monkees tunes, and our first gig was fourth-grade teacher Mrs. Bugden's surprise birthday party. Turns out we screwed up on the date and were five months late. She was surprised.

1967. Saw some kind of rock and roll band play at Expo 67 in Montreal. I remember being slightly embarrassed that my parents were watching with me. I also happened to see my school principal riding the monorail. It's a terrible thing to see your principal halfway through the summer—it only serves to remind you that the summer days of freedom will soon be over. I thought at the time he was following me.

1969. The first year that being cool became really important. Grade seven. I wanted a really hip album for my birthday—singles were passé—but I didn't know anything about albums. I screwed my courage to the sticking-place and asked the toughest (read hippest) girl in school. She suggested *Honky Chateau* by Elton John.

(Maybe she wasn't as tough as I thought.) That's what I got. It remains my most-listened-to album—meaning I listened more to that album in one year than I have ever listened to anything since.

Best slow dance at school was "The Long and Winding Road," by virtue of its length. Considered the song of opportunity at the dance, DJs were instructed by school chaperons to play it only once, and only at the end of the senior public school dance.

1969. First high school dance. Jane Doner took a bottle of her father's rather peasanty red wine, and I stole two beers. We drank all of it in about fifteen minutes behind the school. April Wine was playing. (Somehow I think that was the vintage of the wine as well.)

It was then I think I understood what rock and roll was all about. It was the live event that made the whole ludicrous thing work—being onstage, strutting your stuff, or being in the audience, acting out that tried and true ritual of playing the field. My first experience with alcohol and rock and roll. I would treat both very seriously from that moment on.

1970. I got a guitar. Not without having to pay my dues by playing ukelele for two years first (the shame). But good on my parents, because the guitar actually came at the perfect time in my life. Since I was too young for a real boyfriend and the hours of dedicated time in bed that that required, and yet not willing to stay in and do homework all evening, learning to play the guitar was good for endless hours of innocent chording in my bedroom.

Those early years of high school were probably the last taste of real leisure time I ever had. I learned "Needle and the Damage Done" by Neil Young. (I realized three years later what the song was about.) I learned "Where do the Children Play" by Cat Stevens. And I learned a guitar instrumental off one of Bruce Cockburn's albums.

It was then that my mother told me I was spending too much time productively in the bedroom. (You just can't win, can you?) She suggested it was time to go public with my new guitar. I found another unsuspecting guitarist to play the bass part of the Cockburn song and off we went to perform for the masses in a talent show at the David and Mary Thompson Collegiate Institute auditorium. It went very well. (I was then asked to join the school folk club—the only female member without long hair. )

1970. My first Bruce Cockburn concert. I learned then that the instrumental I had so deftly pulled off as a duet could actually be played by a single guitar. Shock and shame. Back to the bedroom.

1973. Sex, and the first time I heard Bryan Ferry sing. I laughed—on both accounts. I thought Ferry was ridiculous but remained hopeful the sex could be improved upon. Then I heard Lou Reed—he made me nervous. Mott the Hoople, David Bowie, T. Rex, Queen, Emerson, Lake & Palmer, Chicago. Saturdays were spent in downtown Toronto buying funky second-hand clothes and albums. Endless browsing at Master John's shoe store on Yonge Street, where each Saturday would reveal an even higher platform shoe to be coveted.

1973–1978. Made mid-week treks from the wilds of Scarborough to downtown Toronto to go to concerts. I saw everything from Genesis to Rod Stewart to Alice Cooper to Roxy Music. (I had stopped laughing at Bryan Ferry and realized he would be my obsession for years to come.) With regular floor seats at Maple Leaf Gardens, I took more than my fair share of sparklers and toilet rolls in the head.

1976. Moved out of home into a basement apartment in downtown Toronto. Punk hit Toronto, leading to strange evenings at the Crash and Burn Club. Fascinated, but more a spectator than a real participant, I lurked on the edges of the scene and watched as my friends got pelted with beer bottles, spit and occasionally blood. I knew then I was witnessing a real movement, but it was far too aggressive for me to feel a part of it. But for some of my friends, it became their religion, their politics, their way of life.

1978. Finished school, took my first solo trip to Europe, and Kate Bush released "Wuthering Heights." The realization that rock could also sound like this was liberating—it was large and literal and full of theatre. I fell like a ton of bricks for art rock, as well as Europe and the Italians, the Spanish and the French.

1980. The assassination of John Lennon. One of the saddest days ever. I had no idea I would be so deeply affected. It forced me to come to terms with just what he had stood for.

December 8 demonstrated more than any other date in rock and roll history just how personal and powerful popular music can be. Going home to Scarborough to visit my parents that week, I told them about the candlelight vigil I had attended at Toronto's City Hall, the scene around the Dakota, the mourning that was going on all around the world. They thought the whole thing was ridiculous—John Lennon was not much more than a drugged-out hippie who got arrested and pulled stunts like that ludicrous bed-in in Toronto. I have never felt the generation gap so keenly as I did then. I remember thinking, "If they can't understand how I feel about this, they don't know much about me at all."

1983. Along with five other musical misfits I formed a band called The Crowd in History. We played camouflaged covers of anything that struck our fancy, from Peter Pan to the Beach Boys. Our forte was musical commentary, really. "Be My Baby" done punk. "For Your Love" done à la Marilyn Monroe. "My Girl" as reggae. And "Suspicious Minds" in a Peter Gunn mindset. "Surprise and Recognition" was our motto. We cultivated a small, loyal following of musical and media types and quickly realized how awful the life of a band truly is. None of us was thick-skinned enough to truly endure the stupidity and drudgery of the life of a gigging musician, but we had a lot of fun and occasionally managed to earn enough money to cover our bar tab.

1985. Hired as on-air co-host for "The NewMusic" at Citytv. A background behind and in front of the camera helped me get the job, but it was my love of music that really enabled me to pull it off. For the next five years every day offered a new musical highlight as I got to sit down with the greats and not-so-greats of the music world and talk to them about music. I figure that's about one of the best jobs in the world.

## the regular biography

I was born on October 7, 1957, at Toronto Western Hospital, which is at the corner of Bathurst and Dundas, a not-too-gentle area today and not likely a whole lot different in 1957. It has the advantage, however, of being at the back door of Kensington Market, and so, now and again, I think of myself as a kind of female Al Waxman and imagine myself walking down the street with gutters filled with fish guts and rotting veggies and some CBC Italian voice yelling, "Hey Brown—Brown of Kensington!"

My mother assured me that I was her first child. (She had another, thirteen months later, my sister Susan, and I'll get to her soon.) We first lived in a very small apartment at Midland and Kingston Road in a place called Scarborough. All through my childhood, Scarborough was dismissively called "Scarberia" by everyone (a tradition that Scarborough's Barenaked Ladies are trying to abolish). It is a so-called planned bedroom community for Toronto, filled mainly with low- to middle-income houses and apartments on streets with inappropriately idyllic names. Since my parents moved to Nova Scotia in 1980, I have not had much occasion to return to Scarborough, but when I do, I am struck with a sickening, empty feeling in the pit of my stomach that has much more to do with what I feel about the place itself than with my personal family memories. Like those long, rainy November afternoons spent at school, when the boredom level went through the roof and the place inspired me to nothing except sleep. The place was trying its damnedest to make me a member of its lowest common denominator. I consider myself one of those lucky ones who escaped.

My father and mother came to this blessed land from Nova Scotia—Yarmouth, to be exact, where the effects of free trade have shut down the major employers and turned the region into something quite different from the place I remember visiting as a kid. My father is one of the best pianists I have ever heard (someone who Oscar Peterson told me played just like Art Tatum), and he has a lovely bass voice as well. He came to Toronto to take voice lessons and to pursue a career in music and learn to tune pianos. (He tuned Oscar's piano.) After discovering he had intense stage fright, the voice career was shelved (except for church choirs) and he took a job at the T. Eaton Co. (a company with a long history of exploitation of its workers) tuning and repairing pianos for thirty years.

My mother was, all her life, a daughter. Her own mother is an imposing woman of great life-force and a determined nature, who lost her husband at an early age, spent much of her middle years boxing life on both ears with a lot of humour and panache and remains a great and remarkable presence today. My mother started off feeling inadequate and never overcame that feeling. It's too bad, because she was a sensitive and gifted woman who was well loved. But she let her constricted nature torture her into a kind of daily guilt that preyed on her dangerously low self-esteem.

When I was old enough to be conscious of this, I had a weekly example of her particular problem on TV on "The Carol Burnett Show." I saw my mother as Eunice, in the famous "Eunice and Mama" sketches. Those routines were never funny for me, but they served to make my mother's complex nature more transparent and sad. She only found her real self, and her heroic side, much later, while I was writing this book, and while she courageously fought ovarian cancer in her late fifties. Thumbing her nose at the medical establishment, she took charge of what was left of her destiny. She died in 1990.

My own psychoanalysis of my family leads me to believe that because my father's musical career was stunted by crippling stage fright and my Mom laboured under an illusion of inadequacy, by birth and breeding, I had to be an exhibitionist.

Exhibitionism was enhanced by growing up in Scarborough in the mid-1970s, which was when the 1960s hit the burbs. I was a pretty good student but found high school boring. I wasn't good at sports, abhorring anything competitive with lots of rules, but I played trombone in the school band. I didn't give my parents trouble, but early on I adopted an impenetrable defence mechanism in the standard teenage wars—I refused to argue. I let my younger sister, Susan, do all the arguing. I would retire to my room while she turned the household upside down.

My real education happened among my friends. At a very early age I started going out with a beautiful boy of Norwegian background who lived up the street, and whose chief attraction was that he resembled Tim Curry in *The Rocky Horror Picture Show.* Together, we painted a mural of ourselves on my bedroom wall (complete with platform shoes and erect nipples), which led indirectly to my moving out of my parents' house, a semi-detached on a street called Dogwood Crescent, at the ripe old age of eighteen.

By this time my Tim Curry clone had gone on to a life in English punk circles. He returned occasionally to lead a pick-up band called Dick Duck and the Dorks. He has since achieved some notoriety, mainly for his brief stint as Nina Hagen's boyfriend and for a band he had that toured around Europe. (On my travels for "The NewMusic" I would run into the band's poster in dressing rooms in tiny clubs in Hamburg and London.)

In my new basement apartment on Charles Street in downtown Toronto, I hung around with people who had participated in, as I had, the Ontario Youth Theatre summer program, which featured rather bent versions of classics like *Twelfth Night* and *The Snow Queen*. I'd have to title this experience Major Formative Influence, since it got me on stage at Hart

House Theatre in Toronto and really got me started thinking of myself as a performer. While I had finished high school with honours and a scholarship, I never went to university. I couldn't see the point, and my parents, strangely enough, never pushed me.

I started doing some TV. My first part was playing a sixteen-year-old heroin addict and prostitute for a CBC docudrama series called "Drying Up the Streets." (I can tell you my parents were not thrilled.) To pay the rent, I was working as a clerk-typist at the Ontario English Catholic Teachers' Association. I then got a part in a University of Toronto musical. I sang some Gershwin at the audition and the musical director fancied me (partly because of my singing, partly because he had heard I was a nun who acted on the side). Television commercials followed, and more TV, too. (I played the lead in another CBC drama called "Maintain the Right," the part of a union leader who falls for Nicholas Campbell, an undercover cop.)

In 1981 my parents and sister moved to Nova Scotia, ending forever my bi-weekly bus rides back to Scarborough for visits, and I had a new rent-paying job at Citytv in Toronto, editing movies on 16-millimetre film. Meanwhile, the aforementioned musical director and I were living together and singing together in our band, The Crowd in History, which played the Queen Street circuit downtown. We spent a lot of cold nights from 1983 to 1985 stapling up posters featuring the strangest Diane Arbus photos we could find, on the few remaining wooden hydro poles in downtown Toronto. Our band, named after a book about mob psychology and mass uprisings throughout the seventeenth and eighteenth centuries by French sociologist Georges Rude (what a hook!), managed to attract a nice, loyal following.

I did a dreadful horror film, originally called *Deathbite* (now called *Spasms*), starring Oliver Reed and Peter Fonda, in which I died horrifically enough to inspire the occasional phone call from friends who've rented it and are full of admiration. I worked with Jennifer Phipps in a musical called *Baby Grand* that played in Toronto at a dinner theatre for a while, and I did other stuff that never amounted to very much. While I realized that I wanted to be a performer of some kind, the acting field wasn't for me. I couldn't stand the audition process. I hated the fact that someone else, the director, was deciding that I couldn't do the part. I was always the second choice, the less conventional type, the riskier casting decision. And women's parts in TV and film in the 1980s were rarely more than props—no one really wanted a character for their female roles.

In 1984 I did something new. I appeared in one of the first blue-chip-hit Canadian rock videos as "the Girl" in Corey Hart's "Sunglasses at Night." Now this is something that was fairly important to getting me on TV, since an awful lot of people saw it, recognized me and thought it was fairly cool. It includes some glamour shots of me as Hart's jailer (presumably he's in jail for wearing his sunglasses at night), who falls hopelessly in love with him. Sigh. The next Hart video, "It Ain't Enough," put us together again, and in this one I played the farm girl who is Hart's true love. I got to ditch him for a sleazeball city feller who has a car with big fins—get it? Neither of these count on my great achievement list, but I did get paid, and I learned quite a lot about how videos get made, who makes them and the kind of impact directors are looking for. Somehow they made slightly more sense than doing beer commercials, where the crew would spent two and a half hours lighting a cold beer bottle (getting the perfect amount of condensation without obscuring the label), and twenty minutes lighting the people in the spot.

It was because of the videos that people upstairs at Citytv, at "The NewMusic" and MuchMusic, noticed me. Perhaps they believed, as I do, that being successful on TV has far more to do with acting than it does with journalism. In the fall of 1984 two hosts of "The NewMusic" left (one to Much and the other to "FT") and Daniel Richler was left to host and produce. He knew I had an acting background as well as some rock and roll experience, and he'd seen the Corey Hart videos. He auditioned me and I got the job. I was finally in front of the camera because of who I was—not trying to be what someone else thought more appropriate. The strange part about that whole situation was that it had never dawned on me that the job of rock journalist was something I should have been actively seeking out. It was thrust upon me, as most of my big opportunities have been, and I feel slightly stupid and embarrassed that at twenty-seven I hadn't figured it out before some stranger did.

In true Citytv fashion, I learned how to make TV while on air. Everyone saw my mistakes, and Saturday evenings became a time of torture for me. Somehow it was only when the show was transmitted away from TV-land and into the privacy of my living room that the mistakes became obvious. It was an exciting first year. Each week I'd learn a few more rules about this very slippery medium, and each week Daniel and I would try to figure out how to break those rules. (My favourite example was the time we told our audience that "fuck" was no longer considered an obscene word. It was finally included in reputable dictionaries, which we read from, and had entered the English language to such an extent that it had lost a lot of its profanity. We said "fuck" a few times and had a good giggle about it. To TV programmers, that item was the equivalent of a pointed stick in the eye. Maybe that's why we lost our syndication in Saskatoon.)

Next season, Richler left to cover arts for "The Journal" at CBC and Denise Donlon came on board. At the same time, I took on the additional duties of VJ at MuchMusic. Much is live TV, and it comes with a whole different set of rules and a whole different level of stress, too. I soon got used to sixty-hour work weeks, last-minute travel and all-night editing sessions. But the hardest thing of all was figuring out how to introduce the same Janet Jackson video for the thousandth time without sounding too sarcastic. I don't think I pulled that off.

The great thing about City and Much at that time was that I was pretty much able to do whatever I wanted to, as long as it didn't cost anything. Record companies paid for most of the trips I took, and I found myself in interesting places doing stories that weren't what the record companies had in mind. "Youth Culture in Ireland," "The Importance of Pop," "Musicians as Artists," "Strange Days Indeed: An '80s Retrospective"—these were all one-hour specials that I produced (on no money) because I wanted to.

These "idea" stories soon became far more interesting to me than introducing another Whitesnake video. But there was little room for improvement on MuchMusic, where the motto is "Spontaneous and Simple." My ideas to bring more content to Much were dumped on as unnecessary; the videos were what kids wanted, not the stuff in between. So I saved my creative focus for "The NewMusic."

By 1989, I knew there was a change coming. For one thing, I was pregnant, and in TV that is a sure-fire career changer. To give Much and City their due—and they're due a lot—they did not freak out at the notion of having a pregnant woman on TV, which is rare enough in any case, and further, they didn't freak out at having a pregnant woman as a rock journalist and, even weirder still, as a VJ. Remember, female VJs are, by definition, teenage boys' wet dreams and teenage girls' role models, and an eight-month-pregnant one overfills that bill.

My pregnancy wasn't the only issue, though. My vision of "The NewMusic" was drifting away from Denise Donlon's. I had in mind a much more street-wise, hip and offside point of view for the show, while Denise wanted to move it more into the mainstream. On top of that, I was tired of producing TV with no money.

After five years on the show my work had hit a plateau, and to move beyond it would require the injection of a little money into the production budget. I wanted to buy old footage, pay out an occasional location fee to get neato interview locations, hire local artists to paint backdrops for stories. But as Citytv's president and executive producer, Moses Znaimer, told me, "At City we make great Volkswagens. If you want to make Cadillacs, go somewhere else." On Much I felt like all the VJs needed replacing. I felt we were all too old, too over-exposed and too over-used to be credible to that network's audience of teens and pre-teens.

To top it off, I had a knock-down, drag-out fight with station management over the unauthorized use of the name "Laurie Brown" in a commercial by a big junk food sponsor. I lost.

Nonetheless I was offered the anchor job at "Breakfast TV," a seven-to-nine morning show (now being nicely handled by Ann Rohmer), but only if I stayed on at Much. Unfortunately, they didn't offer two salaries to go along with it (this is City's most over-used cost-cutting technique—get somebody who is camera-hungry and ambitious to do two jobs for the price of one and a bit).

That's where I was when, at 7:47 a.m. on Monday, April 2, 1989, after eighteen hours of labour that was all pain and no gain, with my ass frozen from epidurals and the sound of a slight squeak as the blade cut through the abdominal wall, Hadley Dawson Lockwood Taylor, all nine pounds, four ounces of her, one week overdue, with a head of the wildest red hair you have ever seen, was ripped out (with the thwack of pulling your palm off the vacuum cleaner hose) into the rolling world, and changed things forever.

Returning to work was no great hardship. I had spent two months at home and two months in Ireland, and Haddie's father stayed home with her for the next few months. What was difficult for me was coming up with a new attitude to my old job. I had never been a serious-minded rock pig. I had always kept rock and roll in perspective—it's not the cure for cancer. But I now found the lack of criticism in TV rock journalism inexcusable. Most of what City and Much offered was nothing more than pure promotion for music product. I had lost my patience for a lot of the one-hit wonders I was expected to interview. Fortunately, after five months of increasing cynicism and crankiness, a new opportunity knocked.

For the second time in two years, CBC's "The Journal" offered me the position of arts journalist for their show. While their first offer had been easy to refuse (I wasn't ready to settle down yet, and "The Journal" sounded too grown-up for me), the second time around I was much more willing to move on. The thought of broadening my field to dance and theatre and literature, all of which I have great love for, more than compensated for the fact that by moving to "The Journal" I would now have to act my age. Now, not only would I be able to interview only the musicians that truly interested me, I would learn to make a kind of TV that isn't hip but can be understood by everyone. The trick would be to try to explain what was going on in the cultural world to an audience that for the most part wasn't already onside, like the Much viewers had been. I took "The Journal" job in January 1990.

Arriving at the office for the first time was pretty weird. Outside of the arts group, who were kind and welcoming, I was generally ignored. After coming from an environment where the office is the TV studio, "The Journal" didn't feel like TV at all. Ralph Benmergui summed it up for me. He told me that on his first day at the office he'd thought he had taken a job at an insurance company. I also moved from a shop where I was one of the oldest, to one where I was one of the youngest journalists. Men wore suits! Women wore suits! The only suit I wore was a tattooed body suit with a motorcycle jacket. And was this place white! More whites than you could shake a stick at. It was only in leaving MuchMusic that I realized how far ahead they were in the minority mix.

For me, 1990 will be known as the year I became an adult. It will also be remembered as the year of no fun. The delight of having Haddie around was undeniable, but the degree to which she controlled our lives made us quite claustrophobic. Add to that a new job that asked me to fit into a news regime, and the fact that my parents were living with us while my mother, getting progressively sicker with cancer, received treatment at the Falk Cancer Clinic in Toronto, and the result was a fun quotient that was low indeed. In a few short months I had gone from being "the kid" to being "The Mother of Us All," not only to my own child, but to my parents as well.

I used to think being grown-up had to do with the contents of your fridge. If I saw a fridge with coffee cream and milk in it, I judged the owner of that fridge to be an adult. But now I think the criteria for being grown-up has to do with how many plates you can keep spinning in the air at the same time. Letting a plate drop is not allowed—each one is far too precious and important—and all the while you're spinning plates, you're yelling to some unseen boss that you've never done this before, it isn't fair. As we juggled our way through 1990, we wondered, how did life get so serious and so imposing so suddenly? In some ways, adulthood is like a return to the worst parts of adolescence. In my twenties I felt in control, smart and one step ahead of anything life could throw at me, but as soon as I hit thirty I regressed to being indecisive, confused and at the mercy of the world—exactly the way I felt as a teenager. Now, for me anyway, an adult is defined as someone who hardly has enough brain power to keep milk in the fridge.

I was doing a lot of growing up, both at home and at work, where arts was a very little fish in a big newsy pond. The thought that a music documentary could be bumped at 4:00 because of a late-breaking political item was hard to get used to. (I still don't take it very well.) But perhaps my biggest frustration was at the number of stories we couldn't cover. With only one arts story a week getting airplay (if that), there was no way "The Journal" could cover the arts scene. Many important issues and artists fell by the wayside. The Robert Mapplethorpe exhibit closings in the States, the closure of the Ontario Art Gallery, the issue of voice appropriation in Canadian literature—they were left for the newspapers, reinforcing the idea that only 'serious' arts reporting happens in print. In spite of that, the arts programming on "The Journal" was being touted as the best on TV. Sure, what got on was good, what didn't get on was the problem.

Perhaps my biggest disappointment was during the 1992 Referendum campaign. In the final weeks leading up to the vote, when every night the TV was crammed with constitutional bafflegab from self-interested politicians, I had an interview with Oscar Peterson waiting to get to air. It never did get on—arts was thought inappropriate during the referendum squabble. Yet, if ever there was a time that viewers of "The Journal" needed the arts, it was then. Plainly, politics wasn't selling—people turned off and the yes campaign failed. The talking head political scientists had missed the bateau. It wasn't because Canadians had given up on the country; it was because the media/political complex had misread tolerance levels. Canadians define the country in ways pundits and politicians have not yet clued into, and it has a lot more to do with Oscar Peterson and Stompin' Tom than with political scientists, polls, and PR.

Even when there wasn't a referendum, or a war, or an election, or a hockey playoff, the arts were ghettoized to the end of the show, mostly on Friday, as a kind of human interest, feel-good piece. Arts were considered dessert, never meat and potatoes. But beyond the politics of "The Journal," I think there were some great music stories. The reason I had come to the CBC was to be able to make TV that didn't rely on a paid junket from a record company. I wanted a budget generous enough to make sure that every story was the best it could be, and at "The Journal", I got it. I was able to fly to Newfoundland in the dead of winter to make a documentary with Figgy Duff, a rock band steeped in the traditional music of that province. The story started with them taking me to Emile Benoit, at that time Canada's last living mater fiddler and an inspiration for their music. We drank his blueberry wine at his home in Black Duck Brook, then headed down to the community centre for a concert. The audience sat in their skidoo suits and left the cars and skidoos running outside, it was so cold. The story ended with a rocking gig in St. John's on the night of a snowstorm that closed the city. (Even so, the bar ran out of beer.) I was able to go to the Arctic with Susan Aglukark, an Inuit woman deeply involved with the Tapirisat Association. She was a victim of child abuse and a singer in a country band that sings about growing up in the Arctic surrounded by child abuse, drugs and suicide. We followed her to Edmonton for an Oilers hockey game where she sang the national anthem in her native tongue—a first for national TV. It was a music story that said more about the Canadian condition than anything a politician could tell you. Politics leads from behind, while art is always breaking new ground on the frontlines—that's the place to be.

More culture on TV is what I want to see, not simply more reporting on the comings and goings of its most famous artists. Much has been said and written about the ascendancy of "infotainment" programming—the pretense of celebrity gossip as news. This is a trend which is anathema to genuine arts programming and reporting. Arts suffers from all the business exigencies involved in star-gazing. Artists who generally suffer along under conditions of abject poverty can be catapulted into the limelight without the slightest regard for the merit of their performance, but merely on the basis of being good copy, good quote or good viz. Not until arts reporting begins to help people understand what's important, instead of what's digestible like microwave popcorn, will the arts hope to compete with moribund and decaying political coverage in so-called "news" programming.

In August 1992, following the death of "The Journal"'s major doma and guiding light, Barbara Frum, the word came down that "The Journal" and "The National" were to be cancelled and replaced with a one-hour news and information show to be scheduled at nine o'clock every evening. I suddenly found myself working for another show, in a prime-time slot. While the rest of the staff of "The Journal" were mortified by the changes, I thought they boded well. The way I see it, no one could put a news show in a prime-time slot without completely changing the format, style and attitude of the program. If you want to compete with "Murphy Brown," your program is going to have to offer a lot more than "The National" or "The Journal" had done in the past.

When the name of the program was announced, I admit I lost some of my optimism. "Prime Time News"?

I mean, there were five other radio and TV shows out at that moment using the words "prime" and "time." So much for originality. But the fact remained that the CBC had done some testing and had decided that people were really going to bed earlier, and in a television market about to be flooded with new channels (thanks to death-star satellites), the attempt to do something entirely different was to be applauded.

In my mind, we'll have to do something completely different if we want to create a prime-time audience. Not just at the CBC, but at every network that covers the news. Coverage of the Meech Lake Accord and the Referendum turned a lot of people away from politicians and the programs they watched them on. While it was great fun for the political news junkies in TV and their syncophants in print, it didn't make good TV. And at a time when Canadians have said loud and clear through the Referendum vote that our politicians are not believable, not respected and not listened to, most news and information programming continues to use politics as the backbone of the show. Evening newscasts are still dominated by white, male politicians in dark suits and paid experts commenting on their comments. The only thing that changes nightly is the colour of their ties.

I think the Canadian focus has shifted away from power (something "Joe or Josephine Lunchpail" has less and less of), to values and that's what culture is all about. (A case in point: if the Constitution was so all-fired important, why did the issue disappear the day after the Referendum? It was issue non grata in the

1993 election. It was an issue created by politicians for politicians, and Canadians knew it.) All of this indicates we may see more arts and culture on TV. We'll see whether our country's news gatherers, and information and entertainment cognoscenti can handle it.

After taking five months off after the birth of Will (known affectionately as "my last child") on February 10, I was raring to go. Except that Blue Jay baseball games were pushing the show out of prime-time and an election had been called. At a time when music, film, dance and theatre should have been used like great relief pitchers and brought in on every game, there was no room at the inn for arts during the election.

As this book goes to press, the Liberal government still hasn't given us an idea of exactly what they have in mind for the CBC. They promise stable funding so I may not have to live in a stable, although far better women than I have passed the night in such spots. So long as I get to talk more to people I want to talk to than those I don't, I'll consider this a good gig, and one where sometimes I can help remind people how favoured we are to live in such a big, cold, green place. And I get paid for it in the bargain.

On my bureau I have a great photograph by a Japanese/Canadian artist, Nobuo Kubota, which is called "Rock Talk." It's a photo of the photographer himself, with headphones on, leaning over a desk intently, microphone in hand, in earnest conversation with a 10-pound piece of granite. Every time I glance at it I think of the late Frank Zappa's stilletto comment about rock journalism: he said it's "people who can't write interviewing people who can't talk for people who can't read."

That keeps you humble. After Penguin called, suggesting this book, Frank's wise words kept running through my head as I tried to write, constantly fearing that people would think I was perpetrating my minor-celeb showbiz autobiography instead of a book about rock music and television. Well, maybe we can call it the new journalism.

The baby Will is engineering how to pull the power cord from this laptop out of the wall plug. I've tried to stop him and sit him across the room with a vinyl Pooh bear to suck on but he keeps crawling over and looking at the plug like he's planning to rewire the house. Maybe one day he can take a correspondence course on maintenance, like the ones you find on those red matchbook covers at the checkout at 7-11. "Learn TV repair in your own home"—you know the ones. Success without college.

I'll sign off before he pulls the cord and crashes this chapter. Like my old jailhouse PowerHour friends said, stay cool and think free. Maybe more than most teens, they knew the importance of rock music; they had the time to think about it. You should too. We all should. It's worth expending a few brain cells on. Thanks for watching.

January 1994